Champion
of the
World!

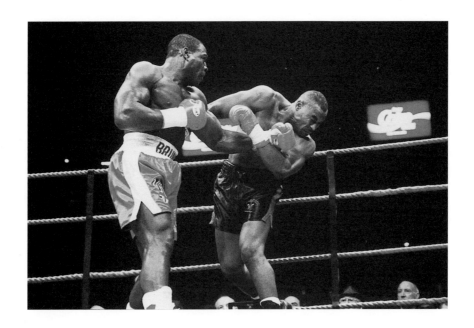

Champion
of the
World!

THE FRANK BRUNO STORY

Malcolm Severs

Virgin

This revised edition first published in Great Britain in 1995 by
Virgin Books
an imprint of Virgin Publishing Ltd
322 Ladbroke Grove
London W10 5AH

First published as Frank Bruno Scrapbook by Queen Anne Press in 1986

A catalogue record for this book is available from the British Library.

ISBN 0 7535 0040 X

Produced by Lennard Books
A division of Lennard Associates Limited
Mackerye End, Harpenden, Herts, AL5 5DR

Editor (for Lennard Books): Caroline North
Production Editor: Chris Hawkes
Design: Design 2 Print
Reproduction: CMYK Graphics Ltd

Printed and bound in Great Britain by
Butler & Tanner Ltd, Frome and London

PICTURE CREDITS

Black and white photographs
Allsport: Trevor Jones 24BL; Bob Martin 110BL, 113, 121, 122-3, 131; Steve Powell 110R; Russell Cheyne 115,
116, 126; Chris Cole 132, 152; John Gichigi 133, 135, 142, 143, 144, 145, 146, 147, 149, 150, 151, 153, 154-5, 156;
Holly Stein 136-7, 138-9, 160; Simon Bruty 118, 140-1; Tim Matthews 148. Alpha/David Parker: 36.
Associated Newspapers: 8, 9, 14R, 23, 33, 48, 51, 61B, 76L, 76R, 87, 104R. Associated Press: 54.
Camera Press: 24T, 82B, 83, 85L. Express Newspapers: 6, 7, 22, 25, 38-9, 42, 44, 69, 71, 77, 80, 90B, 97, 103, 105.
Tommy Hindley: 57, 58, 60, 62B, 63, 68, 72L, 72R, 75BL. Oak Hall School: 12, 13, 16. Popperfoto: 67B, 70,
104L. Press Association: 21L, 84. Rex Features: 10L, 75TL, 112, 157. S & G Press Agency: 37, 46, 61T, 67T, 81,
89B, 90T, 92, 100B. Sporting Pictures (UK) Ltd: 57, 75TR, 94. Syndication International:14L, 15L, 21R, 24BR,
26, 29, 30, 40, 43C, 43B, 56, 59T, 59B, 62T, 64, 75BR, 78, 88, 93R, 100T, 102, 120, 124-5, 128, 129, 130.
Bob Thomas: 18, 19, 34, 35, 66T, 66B, 85R, 107, 108, 109, 110TL. Topham Picture Library: 15R, 17, 20, 27, 28,
32, 45, 49, 50, 52B, 73, 79, 89T, 93L, 96. Universal Pictorial Press: 52T, 53, 86. World of Sports Photos: 74.
Young and Rubicon: 127

Colour photographs: Allsport: John Gichigi and Chris Cole

Cover photographs: Allsport: John Gichigi (front and back bottom) and Chris Cole (back top)

CONTENTS

THE STREETS OF WANDSWORTH

Frank Bruno was always tough but there is something else about him, something about the way he moves that singles him out from the common herd. It is a raw talent, not honed to a nicety in the way, perhaps, of Mohammed Ali, but it is a talent nevertheless — and one that Frank, from his very earliest days, has been keen to exploit. He knew that he was an athlete and that, when he hit people, they had a habit of staying down. He also knew that he owed it to himself to make the most of it.

Frank believes that you only get one chance in life to make something of yourself. His chance was boxing and he took it eagerly. From his schooldays he wanted to be rich, to fly his own helicopter or own his own health farm in the country. He would like to have acquired these things from being a professor or a barrister, but he was no academic. All he had were his fists and a modest ability to ride the other man's punches. They were his passports to a better life for himself and his family, but he knew intuitively that passports expire early unless there is a definite goal to aim for.

Frank's goal was not hard to find — he would shoot for the top. He would be the Heavyweight Champion of the World.

Frank Bruno's early life was tough, not because of deprivation, not because he came from the wrong side of the tracks but because he liked it that way. From the time he balled up his infant fists and punched a hole in his cot to the sound of the final bell at Wembley Stadium on September 2, 1995, Frank Bruno has enjoyed a scrap . . . and it has been his salvation.

As a primary schoolboy Bruno's life seemed mapped out. Street fights, trouble with the law, expulsion, teenage gangs and, ultimately, prison. It was the path taken in life by many of his contemporaries and it seemed to be Frank's destiny until a particularly lucky punch changed his life. At Swaffield Primary School, in Wandsworth, South London, the young Bruno, already very much a heavyweight in the 11-year-old leagues, punched a teacher on the jaw and laid him out. For Bruno it was a simple matter of righting a wrong: 'He was being flash. He used to stand there with his shirt undone half way down his chest, showing off to the girls at my expense. I didn't have any great problems about being black and that but this guy just needled me all the time, so I hit him. And that was that.'

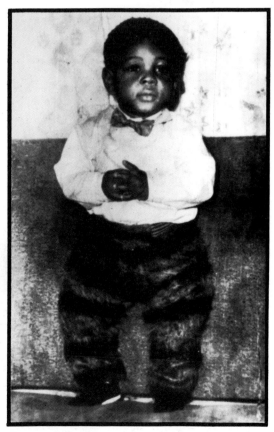

Future champion.

Still 32 years to go till Wembley. One-year-old Frank with his mother, Lynette, and sister Joan, blissfully unaware of the future.

Predictably expulsion followed that punch but the farewell to Swaffield Primary led to an introduction to Oak Hall, a GLC special boarding school in Sussex for difficult youngsters. It was the best thing that could ever have happened to Frank — it was far more a reward than a punishment, although it took Frank some time to see this — and it was the most important single factor in the development of Frank Bruno, heavyweight champion. But it was nearly so different.

Frank Bruno's father was from Dominica and his mother from Jamaica but Frank was born a Londoner in a less affluent area of Hammersmith on November 16, 1961. His father, a warehouseman in a bakery, suffered chronically from diabetes and his district nurse mother, Lynette, had to be the backbone of the family. She worked all the hours God gave to make sure her six children — Frank was the youngest — wanted for nothing. Every morning the children were sent off to school with huge hot English breakfasts of bacon, eggs, sausages and fried bread in their bellies because Lynette believed in giving her kids the best possible start to the day. There often was not enough in the purse for her to indulge in a similar breakfast herself but that did not matter. She wanted her children to grow up big and strong and, with Frank, she was successful beyond her wildest dreams. Her youngest took everything that his mother gave him and converted it with awesome speed into a physique cast in the Rambo mould. Frank was the biggest and strongest on the block — it was a position he had to uphold.

A disapproving Lynette smiles for the camera. Frank's career is set and the family know they can't change his mind. From left, brother Michael, mother Lynette, Frank, sisters Joan and Fay.

The problem, of course, with being the biggest and strongest is that others don't necessarily believe that you are and challenge for the title. Not that Frank Bruno minded. He loved to fight and became undisputed champion of the Hammersmith and Wandsworth streets; a title not relished by his mother. She recalls: 'At school he was a bully boy and I had parents of other boys constantly knocking on my door to complain. I punished Franklin (his mother always refers to Frank by his full Christian name) by keeping him in but he was not evil, you understand. He didn't bully other boys to hurt them. He just liked to fight.'

Whenever the phone rang in the evening and Frank was not around Lynette's heart would sink as she thought: 'What has he been up to now?' But she never had cause for real concern. Although Frank was out on the streets hitting and being hit in return he never found himself in any serious trouble. In his mother's words, 'He was never a problem child. He never got in trouble with the police or anything like that.' But although his mother was saved the agony, so common for the parents of other boys in the neighbourhood, of going to the police station to retrieve her errant son she was still determined to put an end to his aggressive ways. For her the punch that laid the Swaffield Primary schoolteacher low was the last straw. Out of genuine concern for her son she approached the education authorities to see what could be done. During their conversations the subject of Oak Hall was raised. Lynette had no idea that such a school existed but soon realised that it was the only hope for Frank. All her instincts told her to keep Frank

at home as the Brunos were a very close family and Lynette loved having her family about her. But she also knew that Frank was in danger of slipping down the slope to serious crime and she would do anything to stop that happening. Naturally young Frank wanted nothing of Oak Hall. At the final interview before he was accepted he turned to his mother and said: 'But my Dad doesn't want me to go.' It may have been true but Lynette took a long look at her son and said to Allan Lawrence, Oak Hall's headmaster, 'He'll be there.' Those three words changed Frank Bruno's life totally. They were responsible for turning a bruising, swaggering bully into today's quiet, gentle giant of British boxing. They set Frank on his way.

16 stone and well on the way to buying his Mum a Mercedes.

Family boy and houseproud Mum in a rare moment of relaxation.

LEAFY LANES AND COMING OF AGE

The angry punch to the jaw of the unfortunate teacher at Swaffield was, arguably, the most important punch Frank Bruno has ever delivered in his life. That one punch, wild, thoughtless and full of malice, turned out to be his ticket to the better future that he now holds so dear. It led, after a series of referrals and an interview, to a school that even the fertile Bruno imagination could never have conceived.

Frank hated the idea of boarding school. He cried all the way to Waterloo station and the tears continued to fall as the train made its way out of the dirt and noise of London and into the rolling green hills of Sussex. The shock of that change must have been dramatic enough for the young Bruno but the blockbuster shock came at the end of the line when he arrived at Oak Hall . . . it must have seemed more of a palace than a school. If Oak Hall was a public school it would be in the £5,000-a-year-plus league in fees. Set in its own grounds of 80 acres near the village of Broadoak in Sussex, Oak Hall is a country house that still retains much of its original Victorian grandeur. It is airy, with big rooms, and it has all the facilities that some private sector schools would give their west wings for. The difference is that Oak Hall only holds up to 42 boys at a time . . . and those 42 are among the most difficult from the thousands of difficult children who attend ILEA's bleak inner-city comprehensives. Many of the lads at Oak Hall are tough, really tough, and Frank found, on arrival, that he wasn't going to have things all his own way. For the first time in his life he found himself on the receiving end of bullying.

On his first afternoon at the school he knocked on Allan Lawrence's study door. He said he had been sent to the school for education and, as he hadn't been educated that afternoon, could he call the whole thing off. It

was an attitude that didn't last very long. Allan Lawrence says now: 'Frank was biddable, I think that is the term. You could talk to him and, in spite of his own feelings, he would come around and adopt a common sense approach.'

Oak Hall teaches basic subjects but concentrates largely on sports and physical skills. There is no cramming or hard sell learning — just a series of patient attempts to slowly mould something decent from pretty unpromising material. Allan Lawrence again: 'I myself am an ex-Physical Education man and I have a great belief that PE is where we can achieve most success . . . although we do strive to instil something of civilisation and we do aim to turn out reasonably equipped citizens. Frank shone in all the sports on offer here. He was in the Sussex schools' football team when he was a quite junior boy . . . and with a build like his it was the most natural thing in the world. After all, throughout his time here he could always have been taken for two or three years older than he was.'

Just his sheer physical size made Frank a force to be reckoned with in the school and there were times when he gave the staff cause for more than a little concern. There were shaky moments in his development and at these times he was quite obviously the product of his Wandsworth background. As Allan Lawrence said:

> His standards of honesty were not anything like they are now — he developed later. I think he was always aware of right and wrong . . . his mother takes a fair amount of praise in this area . . . but there was a time when we thought he might use his obvious powers wrongly.

From time to time I did have one or two chats with Frank of the "nose-to-nose" variety. I told him in no uncertain terms where he would be going if he didn't watch out. However, I have to say that nothing Frank ever did was terribly serious. But more serious, of course, than if he had been one third the size. You couldn't exactly dangle him from arms length and say, 'there, there, no tantrums'. Of course, it he ever does become World Champion I shall be rather fond of the memory of wagging my finger at him.

The turbulent time for Frank at Oak Hall came when he was about 14. At this time puberty was coming on with a rush and he was particularly worried about the health of his father. One of his more violent moments is remembered by Sandy Nichols, the Principal House Parent at Oak Hall:

One Wednesday afternoon Frank was playing a game of football on the top pitch when he took exception to a decision of the referee. Heated words were exchanged and Frank was finally sent down to see the deputy headmaster. When I came on duty I went into the hall and heard this tremendous commotion — banging, crashing and swearing — coming from the library. I went in to see what was happening and found Frank and the deputy head rolling about on the floor with fists and limbs flailing everywhere. On top of them was just about every book from the library shelves and I don't think there was a single piece of furniture left upright. It was absolute pandemonium. I managed to prise the two of them apart and within quite a short time Frank had calmed down and he soon became quite reasonable about it all. How the deputy head managed to get out of it without injury, though, I will never know.

Shortly after this incident Frank's father died. It came as a traumatic shock and for several months the school had to treat Frank with kid gloves. By 15 however, the worst was over and the hard edges began to rub off Frank very quickly. He became the Oak Hall model pupil and became totally involved with the school. So much so, in fact, that he stayed on for an extra year — he didn't leave Oak Hall until he was 17 — and in that year was virtually an extra member of staff. It was a position of trust that Allan Lawrence encouraged.

He had an enormous amount of easy influence with the boys. He was not a bully, and he didn't throw his weight around, but his opinion was respected because it came from their peer group. Of course, you have to remember that it was patently obvious to every boy that Frank could paste the living daylights out of any one of them . . . but he never did. It was obvious to him that he didn't have to; that he could get anything done by

Pattercake, pattercake, baker's man . . . Frank at Oak Hall where he learned to make real *gingerbread men.*

showing an example. This was a very good lesson for some of our less well intentioned boys who would bully at the drop of a hat. They were able to see that Frank got his way with patience and without fights. However, Frank did develop a kind of special look and when a boy saw it he knew he had better do what Frank was asking, and do it pretty damn quick. It was pressure of a kind, I suppose, but it worked and the boys appreciated that Frank never used his awesome physical strength against them.

One crime that Frank did indulge in until fairly late in his Oak Hall career was smoking. Surprising perhaps, for someone so keen on fitness and body development, but a habit the staff had great difficulty weaning him from. Like most schools Oak Hall has a total ban on smoking — at least as far as the rule book is concerned. However, because of the special nature of the school and the rough, tough attitudes of many of the pupils, the staff did not

Frank (second from right) was mainly a soccer man at school, but he was able to turn his hand to most sports.

worry unduly if the senior boys took a few puffs in the loo from time to time. There were heavy crack-downs if the boy was overt about his smoking or if he tried to sell cigarettes at black market prices to smaller, junior boys. Frank, according to Sandy Nichols, was never in this league but he did enjoy his fag and it wasn't until boxing started to get serious that he was able to give it up.

As well as being a smoker Frank was also a bit of a merry prankster. Cook Kath Lawrence (no relation to Allan and Joan) remembers giving a group of boys lessons in making Gingerbread men. 'You can image my embarrassment when I discovered that the boys, led by Frank, were making their gingerbread men lifelike . . . with all their parts intact. Of course, as soon as they realised I was shocked they got worse. I didn't know where to put my face'

Despite all this, in his final year, when Frank was the closest thing that Oak Hall has ever had to a prefect, he began to involve himself much more with life outside the school. Supremely confident in himself, he would, unlike the rest of the lads who were really only happy in packs, go off by himself to the local disco in Broadoak for dances with the village girls. By all accounts he was extremely popular with them as he was with David Chapman, the owner of White Oaks, a nearby nursing home. Frank had a weekend job at White Oaks — washing up, polishing floors, cutting grass and the like — and David Chapman was so impressed with him and his work that he paid him a cash retainer during the school holidays . . . Frank's first experience of being financially independent.

Not all Frank's experiences at the school were purely physical, however. He was desperately keen on music. The Lawrences arranged for him to have lessons with a piano teacher called Cliff Jordan; a tiny man whom Frank towered over. 'Unfortunately,' says Allan

Lawrence, 'there was no music in Frank. His huge fingers seemed to cover two keys at a time and when he tried to play the piano it sounded awful. He did stick with it, however, and by the end could manage something resembling a tune.'

A common misconception about Frank and his time at Oak Hall is that it was the school that introduced him to boxing. In fact Frank had been involved on the periphery of boxing in his primary school days and had been a member of a boxing club. But it was certainly Oak Hall that helped in the development of the finer points. Unfortunately Oak Hall, because of ILEA disapproval of boxing, was not able to let its lads actually fight. They could have all the boxing training that they wanted — punch-bags, weights, sparring — but they were not allowed to get into the ring to have three, three-minute rounds against each other. It is a rule that Allan Lawrence has always found difficult to understand.

We used to do boxing but ILEA were largely influenced by Dr Edith Summerskill and were against it. In the early days of the school we had a very successful boxing team; before Frank's time. We boxed in the Sussex leagues and once sent a team of seven boys to Brighton and came back with six cups . . . five wins and one for the best loser in the competition. We came out of that hall in a highly euphoric state, revelling in our success, only to meet people selling news-sheets with Dr Summerskill's latest diatribe call-

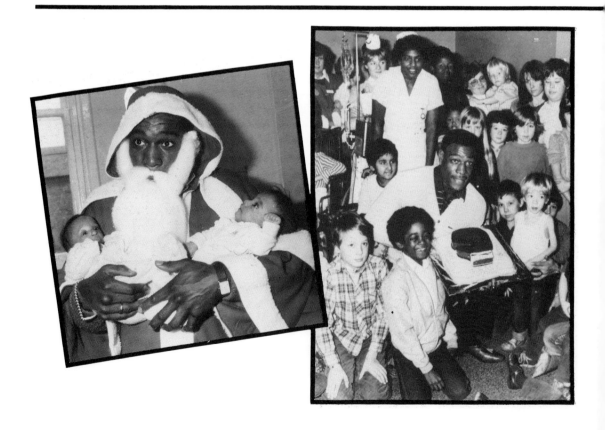

ing on the ILEA to cut out this scandalous use of boys' time. When we had our inspection on boxing I had an argument with the Chief Inspector and I told him I couldn't go along with his viewpoint on the dangers of the sport, pointing out the safety factors built into schoolboy boxing. I couldn't, for instance, equate his antipathy to boxing with his obvious delight in rugby. I asked him if he really thought that a small boy couldn't go into the ring and face another small boy and be tapped about with small gloves but that it would be perfectly all right for him to play on a rugger field where he stood the chance of having half a dozen 14-stone forwards land on him at the same time . . . and all perfectly legal and within the rules of the

game. The assumption was that the rugby boy would get up and walk away whereas the boxing boy would suffer permanent brain damage.

To me it was a nonsense, but nevertheless we have got so many physical activities here that we can quite easily dispense with boxing. If we are not going to be given approval I am not going to fight against it. We shall continue to do the training as we do, and whether they box in rings or not is largely immaterial.

The rule did mean that Frank never had any official boxing while he was here but towards the end of his career we did arrange one or two bouts for him in the area. They were not all successful, I remember on one occasion at Crawley

The classroom was never Frank's favourite place – he preferred the gym – but Oak Hall required him to go through the academic motions.

the chappy climbing into the ring on the other side took one good look at Frank and promptly climbed out again.

Although Allan Lawrence would still like to have boxing at Oak Hall the brutal power of Frank Bruno's punching has led him to moderate his views slightly . . . he is now only too aware of what a Bruno punch can do and he thinks that, perhaps, it was not such a bad thing that Frank didn't get into the ring with too many schoolboys. 'I recently read an article on how hard Frank is able to punch, the speed at which his punch travels, the weight behind it and so on. I have no doubt that he is laying on a tremendous amount of weight in a punch to the head. Certainly I wouldn't like to be on the receiving end of one.'

It stands to reason that Oak Hall will probably never get a boxer of the calibre of Frank Bruno again in its history. Yet while he was at the school it was never felt he would go all the way in the sport. Allan Lawrence's wife Joan remembers Frank as being quite soft.

Frank was always a bit of a baby if he hurt himself. He made a great fuss if he cut his finger . . . not the big tough boxer at all. We all thought that he was essentially too nice, that he lacked the killer instinct. We had another boy here at the time, Gunter Roomes, who was also a boxer. Gunter was much tougher than Frank and he really did have the instinct to go in for the kill. He was a brash bully boy who would have a go at anyone and we thought he, of all people, would get somewhere in boxing. For a while Gunter did become a professional boxer, I think he was also with Terry Lawless, but he stopped and Frank went on . . . and you only have to look at Frank now to see how much he desperately wants to win.

Despite the fact that the Lawrences had doubts about Frank's ability to climb high in boxing it was apparent to both of them that boxing was where Frank planned to go after leaving school . . . and Allan Lawrence was more than a little concerned for his favourite pupil. 'I remember taking him aside and saying, "For goodness sake stay as an amateur for a bit after you leave, at least until you know more about it and can find your way around".' Mr Lawrence believed that Frank should pile up the experience in the amateur ring so that when he did meet some brilliant boxer over the longer professional distance he would be prepared for it. And when Frank took the ABA heavyweight crown his former headmaster knew he had been right.

LEARNING TO HATE WORK

The six years that Frank spent at Oak Hall softened his nature, built his body, set the course for his career and gave him a taste for some of the better things in life. Quite often Frank and staff member Sandy Nichols would go back-packing or rambling on the South Downs and Frank was able to see, close up, the way the affluent live in the country. He saw the large houses and expensive cars that are common in the 'Gin and Jaguar Belt' of rural Sussex and he set his sights no lower for himself. He loved the country itself, he grew to appreciate the smell of fresh air and he had a natural fondness for animals. His problem, of course, was getting sufficient cash to allow for such a lifestyle but the knowledge that the good life was there, ready and waiting as soon as he had the money, stiffened his resolve and fired his ambition.

Back in Wandsworth after his time at Oak Hall was over, however, the real world came flooding back in. He moved back into his mother's terraced house and he began the agonising process of getting a job and settling down again in the less than stimulating environment of urban-decay London. From being a big fish in a very tiny pond at school Frank found himself without work skills in a world quick to exploit those with little to offer. Oak Hall had not been able to supply Frank with any academic qualifications and unskilled or labouring work was all that was open to him: work that was amongst the lowest paid in London.

His first job after school was as a metal polisher. It was hard, he worked long hours, he came home absolutely filthy and, at the end of the week, his pay packet was far from heavy. In addition there was a little mild friction at home because Lynette, like many West Indian housewives, was very house proud, and she became frustrated by the black marks that her mountainous metal-polishing son was leaving around the sinks and the bath.

It was not a happy time for Frank. After the metal-polishing job others followed. Humping bricks on building sites, general labouring,

---

Out of school, the future looked bleak. Frank determined to raise his life through boxing. He joined the Sir Philip Game Boxing Club of Croydon and became British Amateur Heavyweight Champion at 18.

working in a sports store in Brixton . . . they all came and went. He knew from his meagre pay packets that he was never going to get what he wanted for himself by continuing with dead end jobs and he knew, deep in his own heart, that the answer lay with his fists. It annoyed him that he, along with his friends and the thousands of similar people in London, could get exploited so easily by employers. He wasn't in a position to do much for his friends but he knew he had a talent and he knew, if he used it well, it could pull him out of the Wandsworth rut. It was his chance to better himself and he was not going to waste it.

Once Frank had made this decision he could, in all probability, have gone straight into fighting for money. Thankfully, both for him and for British boxing in general, he remembered the words of Allan Lawrence and started the road to fame and fortune in the amateur rings. He joined a boxing club in Croydon and began putting opponents away with all the regularity of All Bran. There was little finesse and little understanding of ring craft but his huge reservoir of raw power was there for all to see. His club, the Sir Philip Game club of Croydon, was respected and successful in amateur boxing circles as was his

coach Fred Rix. Frank Bruno's career in amateur boxing was short and spectacular. In just over a year, and in only about 20 bouts (most going nothing like the distance) he went from a boxing nobody to the Amateur Boxing Association heavyweight champion of Great Britain. In that time he lost only once . . . to Irishman Joe Christle. Joe is now New York based and successful as an accountant but he is still campaigning as a boxer and he remembers his defeat of Frank only vaguely:

I have a hazy memory of beating Bruno because it was just another amateur fight.

It's only now that Frank has gone so far that people are making such a big thing of it, which is rubbish. You are only as good as your last fight . . . and Frank's very good.

On that night I got a trophy and the best boxer of the night award but Frank's a quick learner because when I met him again he caught me with a right. It was a special punch because it ended the fight. I can't remember it.

Joe Christle is intelligent and a keen student of boxing; he has no doubt about Frank's future.

I've been watching Frank's career with interest because people in New York tended to write him off. I've never done that myself. Frank is a very dedicated athlete who trains all the time and is very single-minded. I'm not at all surprised by what he has achieved.

But, in 1980, thoughts of world titles were still a long way off.

Once Frank had the ABA crown there was nowhere left for him to go in three-round boxing and, although he enjoyed winning the trophies and the glory, he was also painfully aware that amateur boxing was useless at putting money in the bank. It was time to turn professional.

Amateur Champion and with his eyes on a professional career, Frank begins to attract the attention of Burt McCarthy and Terry Lawless.

THE BATTLE OF THE MANAGERS

The winner of the ABA heavyweight championship is always a minor celebrity in British boxing, but Frank Bruno more so than most. He was just 18 years old and one year out of school and he had power rippling from every muscle in his body. All the ingredients, in fact, to ensure that sports writers wax lyrical about future prospects. ABA champions are always looked at with a view to the Olympic games and many at the time saw Frank as a likely gold medal winner. But Frank himself had different ideas, he was aiming himself towards the big money purses.

He asked his amateur trainer Fred Rix to look out for a manager for him and Rix introduced him to Burt McCarthy. Frank started to train with McCarthy but, after six months or so, began to look elsewhere and started to train with Terry Lawless in his Canning Town gym. Unfortunately, while training with Lawless, Bruno signed a form of contract with McCarthy. It led to a row between the managers that was to last until Frank fought for the European title against Anders Eklund in 1985. At the time Frank's potential was rated by both managers in the millions and both were very keen to have him in their respective stables — but the ferocity of the row subsided when the British

Burt McCarthy, who Frank left in favour of Terry Lawless and a three-year legal battle.

Still only 20, and now under Lawless' wing, Bruno begins the long road to stardom.

Bruno celebrates as another dejected challenger prepares to take an early shower . . .

Manager/second Dad Lawless enjoys the moment of victory . . .

. . . And leads his man home.

Boxing Board of Control refused Frank a professional licence.

At school Frank had worn glasses — he had been quite vain about them and insisted on gold frames during his last year at the school — and the Boxing Control Board paid close attention to his eyes during the medical that preceeds the granting of a professional licence. To the dismay of the rival managers and to Frank's personal horror, specialists at Moorfields Eye Hospital in London found he had keratomileusis — a very rare form of acute short-sightedness — in the right eye. It was enough for the Control Board and Frank was told he could not fight professionally until the matter was cleared up. The Board's view was that people with myopia (short-sightedness) were more likely to suffer from detached retinas after a blow to the head.

With the exception of the trauma that accompanied the death of his father it was the biggest blow in Frank's life. All his hopes and dreams were shattered. His vision of a place in the country with as much money as he would ever need faded into a new, depressing vision of life in the take-it-or-leave-it labour market of Wandsworth. In that moment his life was back to square one.

But Terry Lawless was no quitter. He disagreed with the medical ruling by the Board because modern laser treatment for the correction of detached retinas had made the procedure relatively simple — even opthalmic experts were saying at the time that the Board needed to adjust its standard on eyesight tests for boxers. Lawless said at the time: 'Nobody is more convinced than I that the Board doctors have done a wonderful job, but on this aspect I think they should reconsider.'

However, the Board ruling stood and Lawless, after consulting the Moorfields specialists, spent days ringing eye surgeons and experts all over the world in the hope of finding someone who could treat Frank's ailment. The result of these investigations was the shock discovery that there were only two surgeons in the world with a treatment — one in the Soviet Union and one in Colombia in South America.

Terry chose South America and, in February 1981, Frank was sent off, alone, to the clinic of Senor José Ignacio Barraquer in Bogota. The treatment, very delicate surgery to the back of the eyeball itself, was carried out by Senor Barraquer himself and then Frank had time to recuperate, with a patch over the affected eye, wandering the streets of one of the world's most violent cities. Life is worth less than a dollar in Bogota's seedy, crime-ridden back alleys and Frank has probably never been in as much danger as he was at that time. With one eye covered he was vulnerable but, more by luck than management, he came out of the experience unscathed and much more grown-up. It opened his eyes to the big bad world and it was largely responsible, along with some sensible fatherly advice from Terry Lawless, for Frank's reluctance to accept people into his inner circle and for his insistence that his private life be kept out of the harsh glare of the spotlights.

The Bogota operation was a success but, on his return to England, he was not immediately granted his much-wanted licence. The Board needed to be assured that the treatment was a permanent success and Frank was required to wait for their final decision. During this time — and with the odds against him being given the go-ahead considered to be somewhat less than 50–50 — Frank continued to train. It made Terry Lawless look at his young protegé in a completely new light.

> What impressed me most during that period was the fact that, for 18 months, when Frank knew he might never get a licence to box, he never missed a day's training. Seven days a week he was at it, keeping himself in magnificent shape. He

TOP LEFT *In the Canning Town gym with Lawless, the shaking by Jumbo Cummings just a few months away.*

FAR LEFT *Thinks: 'Where can I find a big enough man to test my lad?'*

LEFT *Eyes on the future: 'When I'm 25 no one will be able to stay in the ring with me'.*

ABOVE *The wheels of love. Could this be the day he met Laura?*

never gave up hope, never let his dream go. It's from that kind of dedication that you find champions.

He did find time for relaxation, however, and it was during an afternoon roller skating in Battersea Park in 1981 that Frank was introduced to Laura who was to become the special woman in his life. Laura was 21 at the time and worked at a children's nursery but she was not bowled over immediately by Frank's charm and good looks. 'It wasn't exactly love at first sight,' she told a Sunday paper in 1983. 'At first it was no more than a platonic relationship — but things change.'

There is no doubt that Laura's company was a great help to Frank during the long months of uncertainty over the licence. Slowly their friendship developed into love and, by the time the Boxing Board of Control finally gave Frank the green light to fight in February 1982, Laura was three months pregnant. Frank and Laura kept the news of the pregnancy quiet at the time. They did not want to annoy their respective families and their attention was fixed anyway on the flak between McCarthy and Lawless that was regenerated by the award of the professional licence.

Once the all-clear was given Terry Lawless arranged Frank's first professional fight. It was set for the Albert Hall on March 17, 1982. Burt McCarthy, however, would have none of it. He told the press at the time, 'I have the only contract signed by Frank Bruno and it's lodged with the Boxing Board of Control. I'm his manager. Under no circumstances will there be any prospect of Frank appearing stripped for action in the Albert Hall.'

Terry Lawless hit back immediately. 'I've done everything according to the regulations. We've been together for two years now and that's how it will stay.' His view was that the 1981 contract with McCarthy was not binding. However, he made it clear that he would pay

any damages and costs awarded against Bruno if it was ruled that the fighter was in breach of it.

The hearing was before Mr Justice Walton during the first two weeks of March 1982 — only days before the scheduled Albert Hall fight on the 17th. For McCarthy, Mr Charles

LEFT *Laura and Nicola meet the Press and Frank begins his search for a house.*

BELOW *Not an ounce of fat in sight. A still-growing Bruno prepares for his first professional fight against Mexico's Lupe Guerra.*

Sparrow, QC, told the court: 'The fight arranged by Mr Lawless for Bruno is a total mismatch which could ruin the boxer's career at the outset. His opponent is too experienced and this could be dangerous for a first fight. I am not suggesting it is physically dangerous but it could damage his reputation and his professional career. A boxer's first fight is desperately important.' Mr Sparrow asked the court to stop Bruno signing with any other manager and to stop the Albert Hall fight.

Frank and Terry Lawless were represented at the hearing by barrister David Davis who told the court that Frank did not know what he

was doing when he signed with McCarthy. 'At the time of signing he was training in Mr Lawless' gym,' said Mr Davis. 'Frank was of limited intelligence and education and had signed the document after Terry Lawless was run down and Burt McCarthy was built up.' He added that Lawless had paid for the trip to South America and for the eye operation and had stood by Bruno at a time when all seemed lost.

McCarthy was quick to reply. 'These allegations are absolute nonsense. I have evidence that I made substantial payments to Bruno to assist him. I was the first person to speak to him about his professional career when he was introduced to me by his trainer Fred Rix.'

Just two days before the fight was due Mr Justice Walton ruled that it could take place. He said there was no contract between Bruno and McCarthy because the boxer was unlicenced when he signed and did not obtain a licence within the 28 days stipulated by the agreement. He ruled that the only contract in force was with Mr Lawless although he added that Mr McCarthy could win 'substantial damages' from Bruno in a full trial of the dispute because the boxer did not give him first option on the right to manage him when he came to fight.

Frank Bruno met the Mexican, Lupe Guerra, at the appointed time on 17 March and, far from being outclassed as Mr McCarthy's lawyer had suggested, had it all his own way. If it was a mismatch it was in Bruno's favour because he knocked out Guerra after 110 seconds of the first round.

It was such an easy win that Terry Lawless took Frank aside afterwards and lectured him on the sacrifices and dedication that would be required if he was to become a successful professional. Without pulling any punches he told Frank what he would have to give up, how much effort he would be expected to put in and

ABOVE *The photographer had to be quick – Frank despatched Guerra in round one.*

RIGHT *Guerra was hopelessly outclassed. Frank returned to the dressing-room without having raised a sweat.*

how much it would hurt. He told Frank that all his fights would not be that easy and that, to meet the challenges ahead, he must devote himself singlemindedly to the cause and he must leave Laura at the front door and not think about her feelings during his preparation.

Frank was impressed with Terry's 'tell-it-like-it-is' approach and took every word to heart. From that moment he was devoted to Lawless both as a manager and as a man. Together they forged a partnership that was

closer to father and son than manager and boxer. The Guerra fight in 1982 was just the first step but they were standing on it. Above them the staircase to the pinnacle of boxing success looked long and hard, but they were both confident that they were on their way.

The day after that first fight Frank went back to his training and Terry Lawless began to map out his plan of attack on boxing's Blue Riband . . . the World Heavyweight championship.

QUICK KOs AND NICOLA

In Bruno's first year of professional boxing he entered the ring ten times and disposed of five opponents in the first round. Four more ended their fight in the second round and only American Rob Gibbs was able to survive until the fourth round.

But although he was winning, and winning easily, the public and the boxing press were far from pleased. In his third fight, for instance, Frank was howled out of the ring after he had dispatched the big Indianapolis American Tom Stevenson in two minutes and 25 seconds of the first round. Although much of the crowd displeasure was directed at Frank it has to be said that he was completely blameless. He had got into the ring and done everything that could have been asked. The problem was with the opponent. In this particular case the Board of Control was just as furious with the performance of Stevenson as were the paying public.

The Board withheld Stevenson's promised $1,000 purse and initiated an inquiry. They wanted to know why Stevenson failed to get back into the ring from the apron while the referee was counting to ten. It had been a good but not a massive punch from Bruno that had sent the American sagging into the ropes and an even lesser punch that rolled him through the ropes and on to the apron. But once he was there he did an excellent audition for an artist's model; he hardly moved a muscle. He did make a feeble effort to get back into the ring but it was never going to succeed during the referee's count; in effect, he had ended the fight himself. Later, in his dressing room, Stevenson said he put the blame on homesickness, 'He hit hard but I was homesick and all confused. I wasn't concentrating like I should.'

It was a pathetic excuse for a pathetic performance and it raised doubts from all quarters in boxing about the wisdom of pitching Bruno against little-known Americans. Many felt that Bruno would be scarred by the derision that seemed to accompany such fights. Boxing Board of Control secretary Ray Clarke summed up the feeling of the Board when he told the press that he had been authorised to examine the whole question of American opponents. 'There are plenty of suitable British heavyweights,' he said.

But, despite the criticism, Frank's next opponent was also an American — but this time it took Frank four rounds to get rid of him. It was an impressive performance from Bruno and many of the regular boxing journalists began to change their views on the Wandsworth Brown Bomber. His challenger on this occasion was Ron Gibbs and Bruno started uncharacteristically slowly against him. But when he found his rhythm the confidence flooded in and Gibbs never had a chance. When a Bruno right obviously hurt Gibbs Terry Lawless yelled from the corner, 'That's the one — go, Frank, go!' Terry's wish was Frank's command and the big, black boxer moved in for the kill with a calmness that would have been impressive in a boxer with ten times his experience. A quick left-right combination had Gibbs down for a five count and there was another combination as soon as he stood up. Gibbs didn't go down again but his gumshield went and the referee, aware that Gibbs wasn't really sure where he was, stepped in and ended the fight.

The Board's wish to see Bruno fighting British opponents was satisfied with Frank's next bout against Tony Moore from Hendon. Unfortunately it was a bit like putting a twenty-pint-a-day man in the ring with Ali at his best. From the first bell it was obvious to everyone that Moore had nothing that could worry Bruno in the slightest. Frank toyed and sparred with Moore for the first round and then put him out of his misery soon after the start of the second. He was only down for a nine count but

LEFT *Tony Moore on the ropes. Better than Guerra, he managed to last till round two.*

ABOVE *Punches that accelerate from 0–200 mph in one second hurt anyone.*

when the referee moved in to stop the fight there were no complaints from the Moore corner; they knew that their man was hopelessly outclassed. That victory took Frank into the top ten of British heavyweights and the boxing writers were beginning to speculate that it wouldn't be long before Bruno was challenging for the British title.

But Terry Lawless had different ideas. He was concerned that his man was giving plenty of punches but not taking any. He knew that the time would come when Frank would be fighting big, hard men who were more resistant to the Bruno attack and who had powerful counter-attacks of their own. With this in mind Terry and Frank packed their bags and set off for the States with the sole intention of getting Frank hit a few times. Still only 20 years old and very much a novice it is likely that Bruno learned more in the gyms of Las Vegas, Los Angeles and New York than he had in his five professional fights.

In the States he sparred with Mike Weaver, the World Boxing Association's nominee for the championship, and spent a lot of time in the company of Larry Holmes who really was the champion. It was the best experience that Terry Lawless could have provided. Frank said

With no one in the UK in his league, Frank had to go to the US for experience. Here he is eyeball to eyeball with Larry Holmes – the only undisputed Heavyweight Champion of recent years.

---

later: 'I knew they were great fighters but now I also know they are human beings like everyone else. Mike Weaver hit me hard but I also hit him hard. I discovered that Weaver is not all that keen on fighting and I also discovered that Holmes loves boxing but, at 33, is having to ease up and may not be around much longer.'

There were also even more important discoveries. Terry Lawless: 'Another thing he discovered is how big boxing is over there and that it's still growing. There are fights on TV all the time and, with many more subscribers to Pay-to-View TV, it's pulling in more and more money.' Lawless knew that to get Frank into big money boxing it was necessary to become a part of the huge US boxing industry but he turned down the offer of a fight in Los Angeles because he was not sure that Frank was ready. He did, however, arrange to fly Larry Holmes' chief sparring partner Marvin Stinson over to England the following month in order to round off Bruno's training. Getting Stinson to England cost £4,000 but it was money well spent. As Frank said at the time: 'I had a week sparring with him out there and it was great. He comes in, makes you work, makes you move, and I need to do that.'

Not long after Frank and Terry returned from that visit to America an event of crucial significance happened in Frank Bruno's life . . . the birth of his love-child daughter Nicola. Frank and Laura were both delighted but they knew that the addition of Nicola would change the pattern of their lives. At first Frank refused to talk to the press about his daughter and he tried to protect Laura from the non-stop hassle that the Fleet Street tribe are so skillful in creating. He continued to live in Wandsworth with his family and Laura brought the baby visiting every day but it was a situation that could not go on.

Before long, of course, Fleet Street succeeded in uncovering the story and Frank was obliged to wheel Laura and Nicola out for a

Larry Holmes was at the end of his career but Frank was able to see that champions are only human. He learned at this time not to be influenced by the 'superman' hype of promoters.

public airing. In front of the serried ranks of hacks he cuddled and kissed the baby and said: 'Laura and I are very, very happy. We are looking for a home to buy together but there are no plans for marriage at the moment.' When asked why Frank was very specific.

There are a lot of cranks out there and I've had a lot of funny letters from people and I don't want any more. I don't see the colour of a man's skin and I only read the

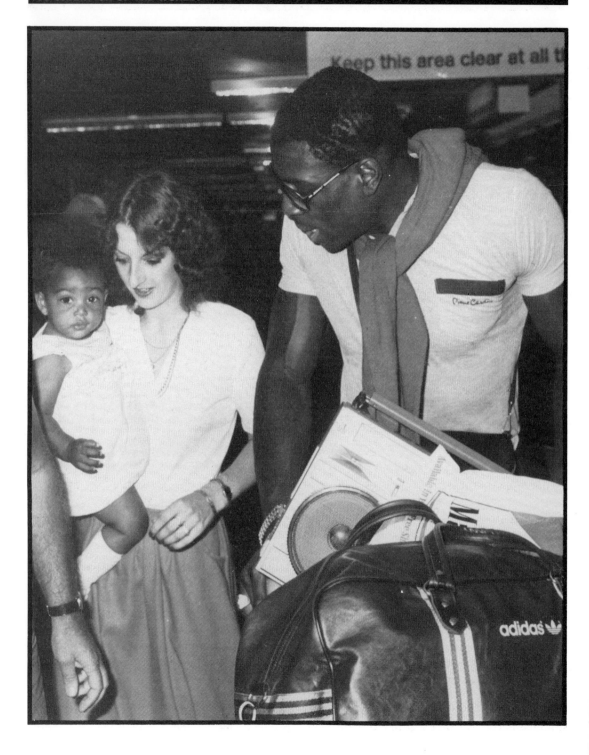

LEFT *Proud Laura and Nicola meet Frank and the ubiquitous ghetto blaster at Heathrow.*

ABOVE *Ninth victim George Butzbach bows to his victor in round one.*

Bible because it teaches that all men are equal, but a lot of people out there do see colour. To them the fact of the matter is that I'm black and Laura is white. But Laura is a very constructive girl. She knows that right now I've got to concentrate on my boxing. There will be plenty of time for marriage later.

Frank and Laura are both religious people and, although Nicola was not a planned baby, they were both delighted when it happened and they resolved to bring up the child together. But Frank was aware that as a boxer in 1982 he was only getting 'office wages'. He wanted the very best for Nicola, including public school education, and he knew that the only way to achieve that was to press his nose hard down onto the boxing grindstone. To people who suggested that Laura and Nicola would take his mind off the job of winning Frank had a stock answer. 'I have two more people to win for now, it gives me more strength.'

And, indeed, as the year passed more fighters came and more fighters went, most only getting a minute or so to size Frank up before becoming more notches on his belt.

The fight with Joe Bugner was to come in 1987.

Belgian Rudi Gauwe managed to last just into the second round, German George Butzbach lasted two minutes before he retired and Costa Rica's Gilbert Acuna incurred the wrath of the crowd by managing to hang around for just 40 seconds. The crowd were livid at this inept performance but referee Harry Gibbs had no choice but to stop the bout even though a wobbly Acuna was saying, 'Come on Bruno, I am very well.'

After the fight Frank said: 'I hit him with a good right hand. It made his nose bleed and his legs were gone. It looks as if I might have to go and learn the business in America again.' Terry Lawless agreed: 'He is ready for any fighter in Britain but those who are willing are asking ridiculous money. It's beginning to look as though we will have to go to America.' Even the Boxing Board of Control joined the general debate. 'The honeymoon is over. Bruno has to have tougher opposition,' it said.

A fine bureaucratic pronouncement. But where were they to come from? The obvious serious opponent for Frank at that time was Joe Bugner and there were talks between Lawless and Bugner's manager Frank Warren. But the talks always foundered over the thorny question of money and who was to get what. Warren, in January 1983, made an offer to stage the fight for £200,000. But there was a major stipulation . . . the purse had to be split 60–40, meaning the loser would get £80,000. Lawless' view was that the winner of such a bout should get more than 60 per cent of the purse and, as a result, the fight was never staged.

So the dilemma remained. Where would Terry Lawless find suitable opponents for Frank? It was a vexing question and it was one that was becoming increasingly important to answer. In a nutshell Frank was not getting the experience he needed. In his ten professional fights to the end of 1982 he had started only 17 rounds. During those rounds he had seen only 38 minutes and five seconds of action and much of that time was spent watching referees count out the vanquished. All Terry Lawless could do was continue arranging bouts for Frank at the Albert Hall in the hope that someone would turn up who could give him a good contest. It was to be some time before that person came along.

CONQUERING CRITICISM

In 1983, as Frank was intensifying his training to meet some of his heavier opponents, he had to face a blistering attack from his mother. Lynette, as well as being a district nurse, was a lay preacher in the Pentecostal Church and she found it difficult to accept Frank and Laura's baby and difficult to accept boxing itself. She gave vent to these feelings in an interview with *All Sport* magazine — an interview which stung Frank and manager Lawless.

In her broadside Lynette fumed: 'Franklin believes in the Almighty but he is still a sinner. He doesn't give his heart to the Lord. He asks for His protection but refuses to obey His commandments.' And on boxing: 'I hate the sport but I wouldn't stop him because a man has to find his own way in life. I just pray before a fight that he won't get hurt and that he won't seriously hurt his opponent. Boxing is a very worrying sport for a mother.' She went on to spell out the difficulties she had had to face when Frank was young. She told of his constant scrapping with other boys and how she'd had to send him to Oak Hall to sort him out.

Frank never reacted personally to his mother's barrage, he was always a private person and it would have pained him more to upset his mother further, but Terry Lawless was furious. Waving a copy of the magazine to reporters in his Royal Oak gym he said: 'It's rubbish. That's all I'll say. I'm not saying anything about it and nor is Frank. Why should we say anything about this sort of thing.'

One of the reasons that Frank kept his personal feelings under tight control at the time was that he understood well the way his mother felt. When he was only about 15 he had told her that he wanted to be a boxer and added, 'When I grow up I'm going to buy you a Mercedes car.' He had his arms around his mother at the time and tears were running down her face; she didn't want her son to fight and she could hardly bear the thought of him getting hurt. Frank told her that he wasn't any good at anything else and that boxing was his only chance to make something of himself and make money. It didn't change his mother's mind but she did realise that there was nothing she could do to stop him. Lynette still hates Frank boxing but the minute a fight is over Frank always telephones her.

> She's never been to see me in the ring, never watched me on television. She just sits at home in Wandsworth with my brother and sister and two cousins waiting for that call. I think she's proud when I win but really she just wants to know if I've suffered. When I lost for the first time she just asked me if I was hurt bad. She never mentioned the fact that I had lost. I was worried that she would be upset by the publicity the next day. But she didn't say a word — even though bad talk about the family has always got to her.
>
> I used to ask her to come along to the fights but now I don't bother. She was against it from the start and she is too proud to change her mind. It used to upset me but now I understand her better than ever. She's a clever lady, much more clever than me. People go to her for advice. She's very religious and has a close circle of friends who think the same way. I believe in God but not like she does. Perhaps I'm the loser on that one.

Lynette still treats Frank just as any other member of the family — she refuses to give him the star treatment — and Frank wouldn't have it any other way.

> I like being in the family. When I go home mum cooks me a great big dinner

and I always wish I could go more often. Deep down I suppose I'd love her to be at the ringside when I fight for the world title and I'm sure she would look at me with the same kind of pride she had when I was little. But I don't suppose she will be there. She's made her stand now and she will stick to her guns, no matter what. Naturally she would much rather I had done well at school and got a job in the bank. Then she would know I was safe. I suppose that's what mums are really about.

But Lynette accepts boxing now — she knows she has no real choice.

Much as he loved his mother and his family Frank knew in 1983 that he had to get a place of his own. Laura was visiting Wandsworth every day with the baby and that was unsatisfactory enough but, once the word got out about his white girlfriend, he started to get verbal abuse while out training from brainless white youths whose only recreation was violent and overt racism. Frank himself could take it. He didn't see colour himself but he understood racists — he had known of them all his life — and he was big enough to let their taunts bounce off his massive shoulders. But Laura and the baby were another matter. He didn't want them involved in any racial trouble and he worried when they visited Wandsworth.

The result was that Frank bought a house in Chadwell Heath near Romford in Essex and he and Laura said goodbye to Wandsworth and set up home in a roomy four-bedroom house close to the forests and heaths of suburban outer London. It was a good choice for Frank because it gave him greater freedom in his training and he was able to run in Epping Forest away from the gaze of the public. It was also, conveniently, very close to Terry Lawless' house. The move put him much nearer to his 'second dad'.

To get around he bought himself a Ford Granada Ghia and equipped it with six speaker surround stereo. Press Association boxing writer Bill Martin, who has often driven with Frank in the car, says the noise in the car is always so loud that Frank would never know if a nuclear bomb went off behind him. He likes to play Stevie Wonder best but Frank has wide musical tastes and often plays opera, especially recordings by Pavarotti. He gets this from Lawless who has a passion for opera. Terry once said that he would have been much happier managing opera stars: 'I can think of nothing better than being surrounded all day by all that fabulous music.'

Being close to Terry Lawless made it easier for Frank and Laura during the last two or three weeks before a fight. In those weeks Lawless fighters always stay in the manager's home where they are looked after by Terry's

tiny wife Sylvia. Sylvia is just 5 feet tall — the top of her head at about the same height as Frank's chest when they are standing together — but she was adored by all Terry's fighters . . . and especially by Frank. They went to the Lawless home to keep them away from domestic pressures and to give them a couple of weeks of uninterrupted training. 'It's not just to keep them away from women,' said

BELOW *Sylvia Lawless, Frank's 'Mum' and minder before a fight, serves a modest snack.*

RIGHT *Two champions in their own right. Frank eyeballs a one-ton prize bull – about a year's supply of breakfast steaks.*

Sylvia. 'If they're serious about their training they do that anyway. It's to keep them away from the problems of life. They tend to get at their wives when they're near a fight, it's only natural. Here they are protected from all those problems. If they have worries they can't do so well in the ring so Terry spends a lot of time here cheering them up.'

In order to make the move to the Lawless house as painless as possible Sylvia created a homely atmosphere and told the fighters to treat the house as though it was their own. It was an atmosphere that Frank appreciated. 'She looks after me better than the Hilton. I don't like hotels much but I like staying here. She tells me off sometimes — like if I come in with dirty shoes or something — but she does all my washing and she's a great cook.' Sylvia took great pride in the success of Terry's boxers and she never missed a fight, at home or abroad. And she had a particular soft spot for Frank. 'Frank is an example to other kids to make something of themselves. After his last win I answered about 400 letters from fans including one from a boy who said, "Thank you for showing me that with hard work and dedication anybody can be anything".' It was the sort of letter that helps to spur Frank on. To this day he is at his happiest when he thinks he is being a real help to people.

Having Big Frank in the house, though, was not a pleasure that could have been afforded by the average British household. For breakfast Sylvia supplied a pound of best steak, four rashers of bacon, two sausages and a couple of eggs — plus all the usual breakfast trimmings. And for the evening meal there would be a huge lasagne to start (one of Frank's favourite meals) followed by another steak with four vegetables and potatoes and fresh fruit and ice cream to finish up. At the end of it all there would be nothing left on the Bruno plate — lack of appetite has never been one of Frank's failings and although he has always been a prodigious eater there has not been a surplus ounce of fat on his body for ten years.

The first eight fights of 1983 followed pretty much the same path as the over-in-a-flash fights of 1982, except they tended to go on just a little longer: the average lasting just a fraction under three rounds. Even so the boxing public was far from impressed.

The first fight of 1983 should have ended in the first round but it took Frank until round four to dispatch Stewart Lithgo of Hartlepool. Lithgo was nearly two stones lighter than Frank and was a very thin man for a boxer. He had three more years' experience than Frank but limited abilities yet he managed to use

what abilities he had to make Frank work for his money. The second round was actually shared as little Lithgo ducked and weaved and caught Frank napping with some perfectly timed forward attacks. By the third round Bruno had sussed out Lithgo's thinking and got in a devastating hook to the head which opened a large cut in Lithgo's left cheek. It was sufficiently bad for his manager Dennie Mancini to call it a day and end the fight; a decision bitterly resented by the plucky Lithgo who had to be dragged away from the ring protesting that he wanted to go on. But Lithgo needed three stitches to a left eye cut and two to another cut near the right eye. To have gone on would have been suicide.

LEFT *Plucky ex-jockey-cum-boxer Stewart Lithgo lasted four rounds against Frank.*

ABOVE *Smiles from African Peter Mulendwa. He had the smile wiped off his face in round three.*

The next fight was no better. It was a hastily arranged affair against Ugandan Peter Mulendwa at the Albert Hall and it had the crowd booing when Frank ended the fight with a third round knock-out. It wasn't that they were booing Frank's performance — on this occasion he did everything that could possibly have been asked of him — it was that the paying public were getting fed up at not getting their money's worth. Mulendwa, again nearly two stone lighter than Frank and more than six inches shorter, put up what resistance he could (mainly crouching low to give Frank the smallest possible target to hit) but he was never any match for Bruno and the third round left hook that ended it had been predictable from the first bell.

Frank was as frustrated as the fans and he went over to help Mulendwa at the end of the fight. Lawless, on the other hand, was pleased. His view was that Frank, for the first time, had done nothing wrong. Lawless insisted: 'He was relaxed, took his time and picked his punches . . . and that body punch would have

ABOVE *Winston Allen scores – but not for long. The referee stopped the fight in round two.*

RIGHT *A cut above the eye put paid to Eddie Neilson's chances in round three.*

finished anyone.' But although the fight pleased Terry he knew, just as the public did, that Frank needed tougher opposition. The problem was finding it.

It wasn't found in the next bout — Welshman Winston Allen could stand for only a round and a half — but his fourth fight of the year, although still short, had the crowd on their feet cheering. Against Swindon's Eddie Neilson — a man every bit as big as Frank — he put on a display of aggressive boxing that had the crowd yelling for more. It took him

two rounds and 25 seconds to leave Neilson bleeding and bruised on the canvas — half the time it had taken Joe Bugner to stop the same opponent five months earlier.

The crowd hated Bugner and booed him when he took up his ringside seat; they would have liked nothing more than to see Frank pounding the cocky Bugner into submission. Frank wanted it too but Terry Lawless was content to bide his time — he still felt that Frank was too raw. This view was echoed by the beaten Neilson who said after the fight:

Scott Le Doux (LEFT) *gets a leg up . . .*

. . . And a hand out (ABOVE).

'Bruno has a lot to learn and I think Bugner would win because of his weight and experience.' Even so the public had seen with this fight that Frank had the aggression and the equipment to win a major contest, and Frank knew it. 'I should have finished him in the first round,' he said later, 'but that will come with experience. You ain't seen the best of me yet. Terry was telling me to box him but because of the comments he made before the fight I wanted to destroy him. Still I did what Terry said and slowed down, boxed and picked my punches. I'm learning all the time.'

And so he was but it didn't stop the popular joke in boxing circles at the time, 'When Bruno's fighting there ought to be a money back guarantee for people who blink.'

In May Frank faced the biggest test of his career with a bout against American Scott Le Doux — a man who had been in with five world champions and who had fought for the title himself. Former champion and New York Boxing Commissioner Floyd Patterson was at the Wembley ringside for the fight and he said of Frank after his typical three-round win: 'This man can go all the way.'

Bruno was as dominant in this fight as he had been against any of his previous opponents and it impressed Le Doux himself. 'I rate him,' he said, 'among the top five punchers I have met — certainly better than Larry Holmes or Leon Spinks.' Frank was proud of that comment and proud of his performance. 'I was under a lot of pressure and he tried to psyche me out. He was pretty tough and knew all the tricks of the trade. Still, it would be nice to go the distance sometime and see what happens.'

But the most satisfying comments after that

fight came from Floyd Patterson himself. Floyd had been brought over by Lawless to give Frank advice and to help him in the Canning Town gym. He worked on Frank's jab, concentrating on making it quick and sharp, and, more importantly, he gave Frank the benefit of his years of experience in big-time boxing. And after the Le Doux fight he was full of praise for Frank.

What I like best about him is that he learns. I've worked hard on that jab and the way he used it was tremendous. He's the most exciting prospect I've seen for years. Give him two or three years and 20 more fights and he could well become champion.

TOP *Former Heavyweight Champion Floyd Patterson makes his point at a Bruno training session in Canning Town.*

LEFT *Terry Lawless spared no expense to get the best possible advice for his potential champion, and they don't come better than Floyd Patterson.*

The great thing about him is that he doesn't get excited when he hurts a man. Most people start flailing when they have someone in trouble but Bruno stays cold. He is unbeaten, and that's good, but the most important thing he has to learn is how to lose. He's got to know what it's like to be knocked down and to force himself to get up again to win. He's got to learn how, when he gets hit, not to show it. He's got to learn that when he does lose it isn't a tragedy. Losing can be the beginning and not the end.

Terry Lawless was delighted with Floyd's advice. 'Floyd was not only a great champion but a perfect gentleman and there could not be a better example for Frank to follow.' What he didn't know was that the lesson of losing wasn't so very far away.

FLOYD'S LESSON LEARNED

After the Le Doux fight Peter Moss of the *Daily Mail*, the boxing writer who knows Frank Bruno ·best, was surprised that the crowd booed for a few minutes, angry that they had had only seven and a half minutes of entertainment. 'But when Bruno bowed to them with genuine respect the cheers took over to drown the dissent. They admire him, more than that, they like him. The big black kid has grabbed them the way Henry Cooper still does and the way Joe Bugner never could. And what a breakthrough it is that his colour does not matter.'

Frank was pleased that he had the love of the crowd but Terry Lawless was much more matter-of-fact about it. His job still was to find Frank fights that fitted in to his master plan for the final assault on the top of the hill. And he soon realised that, to find that fight, Frank was going to have to go back to the States. And this they did, in July, to fight big Californian Mike Jameson in Chicago.

It was worth the trip, Frank put up one of the performances of his life. He stopped Jameson in one and a half rounds and he was ecstatic. 'I believe I could go out and win the

world championship tomorrow,' he crowed after the fight. He believed it and so did the British fight followers who watched the fight, either at ringside or at home on television. Frank had won in style, he had supreme self-confidence and the win had elevated him from heavyweight prospect to heavyweight contender for the title. Even Terry Lawless was delighted. He told Peter Moss after the fight:

> Our relationship has changed. I told Frank that I'm not the governor any more. We are now partners. What Frank did out there was the best heavyweight knock-out I've seen. It was how cold he went that impressed me. He hurt the man with his left hook but found the right position to throw the right which made sure it was all over. Anybody in the world hit by punches like that would have had to go.
>
> He may be right about winning the title tomorrow, certainly a couple more wins, maybe only one, will put him in a position to challenge. But merely fighting for the title is not the target at all. When he goes in there I want to be sure he can not only win it but keep it for a long time.

Frank was in full agreement with this approach, indeed he politely declined Terry's 'partnership' offer.

> A partnership's all very well but I'll still wait for Terry to give the word. He's the man that has produced four world champions. I'll trust him to know when to make the move. But for two weeks here I've mixed with guys in the gym and I've more than held my own. I didn't know that they were world rated but it has

LEFT *Frank's first fight in the States left burly Mike Jameson out cold.*

made me realise there is less of a gap. My part in the partnership will be to build up my body and my punches and my experience so that, when Terry says go, I'll be ready for the fight of my life.

As well as impressing British boxing fans the Jameson fight had the name Bruno buzzing around the gyms from coast to coast in the States. Jameson said after the fight: 'He's a real nice guy and he's going places. Nobody ever hit me like that.'

But perhaps more importantly he impressed one of the great pillars of American boxing, former Mohammed Ali manager Angelo Dundee. 'The kid is built like a brick outhouse with all the bricks in the right places. When the chance came he produced the left hook from nowhere and he poleaxed the guy with the right.' But Dundee, a wily old ring craftsman, had criticisms too. 'His back foot was wrong. It was going east to west when he was going north to south. Then there is the way he walks forward instead of sliding. Somebody could hit him in the middle of a walk and knock him cold.' They were wise words from Angelo and they were the first indication that there was anything seriously deficient in Frank's boxing armoury. They went largely unheeded.

Frank was still only 21. He had had 17 professional fights and all had ended in knock-outs well inside the distance. He was a celebrity. On his return to Heathrow he was met by rapturous fans, equally rapturous press and by Laura and Nicola, then just 11 months old. Laura was deliriously happy. She, along with millions of others, had watched the fight on television. 'It was a marvellous performance by Frank. I was glued to the set, it was the best I've ever seen him box,' she told pressmen as she hugged Frank in welcome. And Frank beamed at all the attention. It was the high point in his career and he was enjoying it. He knew that in boxing you had to enjoy your moments as they came, he also knew that his hardest tests were still to come.

There was a short break after the Jameson fight followed by a lightning first round knock-out of Bill Sharkey at Wembley in September. This was to have been a solid curtain raiser for a planned fight against Floyd 'Jumbo' Cummings at the Albert Hall on October 11 but Sharkey bit the dust far quicker than most commentators had expected and Frank was left just gym work and sparring to build up for his meeting with Cummings.

And Jumbo Cumming nearly put the Bruno streamroller into reverse. At the end of the first round Cummings — a burly American only three pounds lighter than Frank who had acquired much of his fight knowledge during a 12-year term at Stateville maximum security prison in Illinois — caught Frank with a punch

ABOVE *New Yorker Bill Sharkey lasted precisely two minutes and eight seconds at Wembley in September 1983.*

to the jaw that would have finished most heavyweights on the spot. Fortunately he was saved by the bell and, despite being almost out on his feet and with legs wobbling like a good jelly, managed to make his way to his corner unaided by Lawless.

Terry immediately looked into his fighter's eyes and satisfied himself that they were clear. He then asked Frank what round it was. He got the correct answer — indeed Frank was surprised that Terry should ask such a 'stupid' question. Satisfied that there was no serious damage Terry got to work furiously to revive Frank sufficiently for the next round. He did a great job but Bruno went out into round two not in a fit state to fight someone as determined and as tough as Cummings.

But Frank would not give up. He summoned up every ounce of strength and courage that he could muster and he used his feet to deny Cummings the chance to capitalise on his earlier fortunate punch. It has to be said that if Frank had not been so supremely fit and Cummings so obviously unfit, the fight would have been over in the second round. Had the roles been reversed Bruno would without question have finished Cummings off with one well-placed combination salvo. As it was, with the Albert Hall crowd cheering its support with every punch, Frank slowly fought his way back into the match. By the fifth round he was on top again and in the seventh Cummings had no answers left and went the way of all other Bruno victims . . . to the floor.

It was without doubt Frank's hardest fight. From the start Cummings had been in no mood to let Frank dominate the bout and Bruno had to work hard, and with perhaps not the clearest of heads, to carry it off. It was impressive and it answered many of the unanswered questions

RIGHT *Almost Frank's first Waterloo. Jumbo Cummings nearly stopped him early but he came back to win in round seven.*

that had been posed by boxing writers over Frank's short career . . . how would he react when he was hurt? . . . did he have the mental fortitude to suss out an opponent when he was not on top from the very first bell?

Frank was certainly hurt in this fight. Apart from the sledgehammer blow to the jaw that so nearly knocked him out he was also cut above the left eye so badly that he needed six stitches after the fight. That cut was sustained in the fifth round but it was completely ignored by Frank. By that stage of the fight he had his eyes

so finely focused on winning that a small cut was completely irrelevant.

The *Mail*'s Peter Moss summed up the feelings of all boxing journalists to Frank's sterling come-back from near defeat: 'To come back from that was the most significant step yet in

---

OVERLEAF *Terry Lawless checks Bruno's eyes after the near-catastrophic Cummings punch. Although rocked, Frank never lost his bearings and slowly got his act together to the delight of the crowd at the Albert Hall.*

the moulding of the man who could be the first from Britain this century to win the greatest prize in sport — the heavyweight championship of the world.' His view was shared by the nine million viewers who had seen the fight live on television. To many of them Frank was the champion already.

When he and Laura turned up at their favourite restaurant, the Trattoria Parmigiana in London's East End, at one in the morning, everyone present stood and cheered . . . and they kept cheering as Frank proved there were no ill effects by enthusiastically downing a mountain of lasagne and a couple of Desperate Dan sized steaks. Later Frank talked about the fight as a 'strange and weird' experience.

> The trouble was I lost concentration for a split second and glanced towards my corner. I didn't realise at the time I had done that but I've watched it five times on video and that is where I went wrong. As soon as it happened I thought to myself 'what an idiot', but there was no question of the lights going out or anything like that. I knew exactly what was happening. I knew the bell had gone and that he hit me again, on the neck, after it. The main thing is to make sure I never get caught like that again.

Next came Walter Santemore — another big American who had beaten Ernie Shavers on points — and, despite a huge pre-match build-up, could manage just three rounds and fifty seconds. Bruno was helped by the fact that Santemore cut easily but it was still a very

LEFT *Bruno jubilant after the hard work of the Cummings fight.*

TOP *Walter Santemore shapes up . . .*

. . . for a round-four knock-out (BELOW).

agreeable way to overcome the near fiasco with Cummings.

In March Argentine champion Juan Figueroa was on his feet for only 57 seconds. It was Frank's seventh win within the first round and the second fastest of his career. And in his 21 fights he had only spent 52 rounds in the ring. A week before the fight Frank had seen Tim Witherspoon and Greg Page fight for the world title and it made him feel good: 'It boosted my morale. All I need is experience and I'll knock them both out the same night.' Good fighting talk but Frank was not getting the experience. Even he had to admit to more frustration than elation after Figueroa. 'It finished too early for me. Sixty-seven seconds (including the count out) was not enough after the ninety rounds I sparred in America. Before the fight I was so anxious to finish it but when it was over I thought "what a pity".'

And so he should have because the next fight was to be the big one in every way — against 17-stone James 'Bonecrusher' Smith. The days of third-rate opponents were well and truly over.

Bonecrusher was everything his nickname suggested. Well up the rankings of world heavyweights, and with a reputation for despatching opponents with almost the same speed as Frank, he was to be Frank's big test before a planned September bout with former world champion Mike Weaver. He was a big leagues boxer and the British boxing public were to have their first chance to see their hero

Argentinian Juan Figueroa was one of Frank's quickest victories. It took just 110 seconds for the man from Wandsworth to land a mighty right and leave the South American to the snipers of the Press corps. The crowd booed because they hadn't had their money's-worth, but Frank had done his job – he could do no more.

fight someone from near the top of the tree. If Bruno could win this one the way was wide open to the championship. Everyone knew it — Frank himself, Terry Lawless, the fight fans, the sports writers and the boxing administrators — they all knew that this was the watershed: this was the one Frank had to win.

All this didn't go unnoticed by Frank and there was tremendous pressure on him from the time the fight was first announced. He was as fit as he had ever been and he was sure of the power of his punch but he knew he was lacking in ring mileage and he, together with Terry Lawless and his trainers, piled on the sparring rounds to build up stamina. When it came time to get into the Wembley ring no fitter man than Frank Bruno had ever stood in a boxing corner. Under the lights his muscles — and they seemed to bulge from all over his body — flashed Morse messages to the crowd. If he had been a racehorse he would have won the best turned out prize by a dozen lengths.

In the fight Bonecrusher was a dogged opponent with a tight defence but Frank was getting his shots in with increasing frequency. He was ahead on round one, round two and round three — clearly ahead on points — and the crowd were waiting for the usual Bruno flurry and a prostrate Smith in the fourth or fifth round. It didn't come. Frank kept winning rounds but he could not find the punch to put the Bonecrusher away. By the last round, the tenth, Frank had won all of the other nine and only had to finish to win. But he paid the price of inexperience. Instead of coasting to the final bell and staying out of trouble he went all out for a knock-out win. It gave Smith his chance. A left hook stunned Frank and his defence dropped. Blows began to rain on him and another left hook had him down in a neutral

corner. He tried to get up but the effort was too much and referee Harry Gibbs counted him out.

Amazing scenes followed. Smith's cornermen leapt about in delirious frenzy and Smith himself lay prone on the canvas unable to believe what had happened. Bruno got up, in full control and with remarkable dignity, and walked across to congratulate Smith. He even appeared to plant a small kiss on the Bonecrusher's cheek. There was a poignant moment as Frank bowed respectfully to the crowd — an action they had seen before only from a victorious Bruno — and then he was gone, quietly, back to his dressing room.

He was philosophical about the defeat: 'Perhaps the occasion got to me. I just got caught, didn't I. Okay, so I got beat. Ali got beat, Frazier got beat and they all came back, and so will I.' But Terry Lawless was shattered. He was in tears after the fight and it was as though his world had come to an end, and not Frank's. He took it so badly, in fact, that he said to Frank: 'You'll have to find yourself another manager.'

Lawless was 50, he was the best and most successful manager that British boxing had ever seen but, on the night of the Bonecrusher defeat, he retired. He told Frank: 'That's it, I can't take any more lumps being knocked off my life.' Throughout his career Lawless had always involved himself personally with his fighters. He always shared their joys and he always felt their pains . . . sometimes more

LEFT *James 'Bonecrusher' Smith plays games for the Press before the 1984 fight.*

OVERLEAF *Bruno outboxed the Bonecrusher for nine and a half of the ten-round fight. He had only to stay out of range for certain victory. But over-confidence and the desire for a knock-out gave Smith the opening for a match-ending punch. At last Frank had learned the Floyd Patterson lesson.*

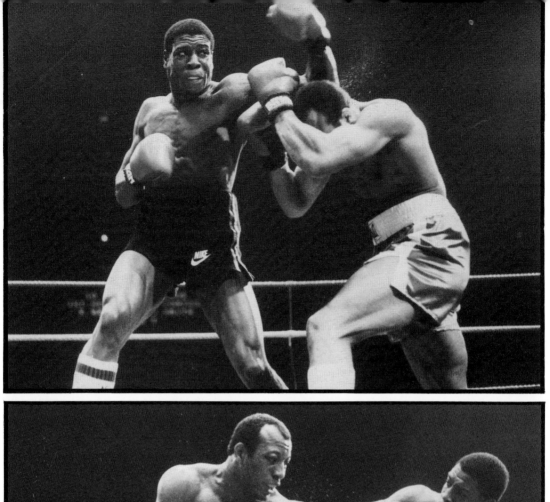

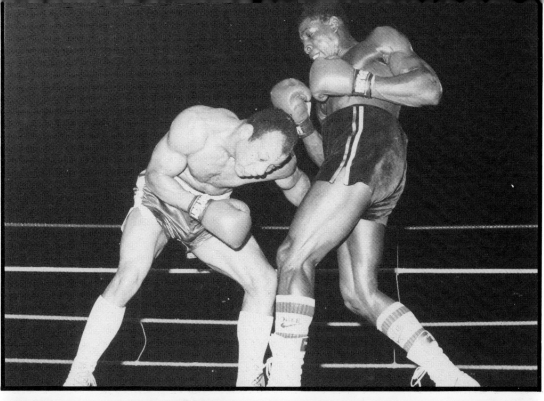

The moment of truth: 'Losing was worse than being divorced from a wife you loved'.

than they did themselves. On this occasion he had had the stuffing knocked right out of him but when he told Frank to find another manager the boxer calmly replied: 'In that case I'm retiring too.'

But the following morning Frank telephoned Terry at his Essex home. 'At the time,' said Lawless, 'I was lying in bed with the sheet pulled over my head. Frank wanted to know whether I was ready to go with him to the post-fight press conference. What could I say? If he had the guts to face up to the situation how could I not go along with him.' With the clearing blast of reality that always comes the morning after a major sporting event boxer and manager became reunited . . . friends, partners and ready, once again, to learn from

the mistakes and continue their positive quest for the world title.

The trouble was, said Terry Lawless, that Frank's record of 21 fights all won inside the distance was 'a curse'. 'They gave Frank the world number nine rating but there was no way I saw him as the ninth best heavyweight in the world. At least this has given us the chance to take another half-dozen fights before we get back to this level.'

Frank had learned Floyd Patterson's lesson well and he had seen a ten rounder almost to the end. The experience he so desperately wanted was at last beginning to arrive.

BODY BEAUTIFUL

Highly tuned bodies like Frank Bruno's are best likened to highly tuned racing cars; to keep going at optimum efficiency requires constant monitoring, expert maintenance and skilled direction. In Frank's case the direction — the best in the business — came at that time from Terry Lawless, the maintenance from trainer Frank Black and the monitoring from Frank himself. Together they had to go through all the work-shop routines and then Frank had to road test himself to make sure everything was buzzing sweetly and all the parts were in synch.

It was a daily routine, as Frank believed if he lost a day some other fellow won a day. The enemy who was trying to destroy his dream was constantly on his shoulder, scrutinising him for weaknesses, for moments of self doubt, for a lessening of the drive to win. Frank was determined never to let his unseen enemy find what he was looking for. There was no let up in the Bruno campaign.

He really was the totally single-minded sportsman with a Holy Grail goal to reach for.

His dedication, however, also came from an awareness that boxing is a business, not a pleasure:

> It's a business, you know. Anybody who has got the bottle to go in there, even if it's like your brother, when round one goes you've got to dislike him. Because where money's involved you try and hate the other person so you can better your own life. And if people are going to get hurt, they are going to get hurt, it's all part of the business. I don't feel bad about hurting a person because he wouldn't feel bad about hurting me . . .

A single-minded Bruno acknowledges the salute of a fellow jogger. Bruno ran more than 50 miles a week in his quest for boxing's most prized crown.

we're both just doing our job. In fact I've never really liked boxing. But I've always known it's the only way for me to get the things I want. If everything goes according to schedule I'll retire at about 28 or 30. There will be plenty of time to catch up on the things I am missing out on now.

Bruno always lived, slept and ate boxing. He had no other job, with the exception of panto and TV advertising, other than boxing and he gave it literally everything he had got. His ten-stage daily training routine began in the early hours with roadwork in Epping Forest. He ran seven miles on weekdays but more at weekends . . . 'I ran 18 miles in two hours 14 minutes last Sunday so I move okay for a man over 16 stones.' One of his running companions was featherweight boxer Jim McDonald, a man who had won prizes for cross country running. He was able to leave Frank behind when he really put his heart into it, but not by much. The run was followed by a drive home (Frank has always loved driving) and a work-out on the speedball he had set up in his garage gymnasium. Then he donned weighted wrist and ankle bracelets, and sometimes a lead-weighted waistband, before taking his Doberman 'Bomber' ('because he lets off a few every morning') for a stroll.

After all this there was an hour in bed ('I love my bed') before driving to the Canning Town gym. On arrival he would sit down and watch the others working to get himself in the

Ordinary sit-ups aren't enough. The weight on the stomach is just to make it harder.

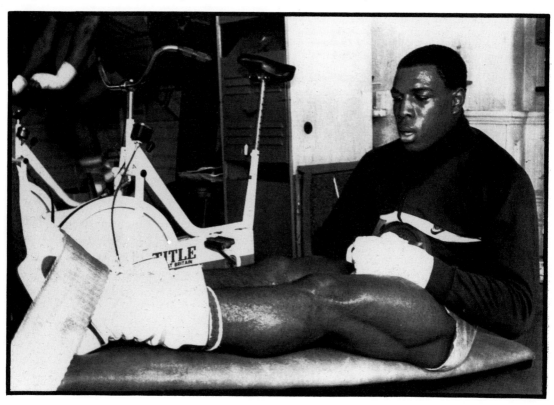

mood and then he would rub his whole body down with cocoa oil before starting his own work-out. 'I watched Mexicans do it in the States. It's good for the skin and it makes me feel sleek and supple. Terry said it's all in the mind but if I think it's good then it must be good for me'. Once oiled up it was sparring time and he would get into the ring with Gary Mason, a man so similar to Frank in appearance that it was only possible to tell them apart by size as Gary was even bigger than Frank! Gary, unfortunately now retired on medical grounds, was a fast boxer who moved well and Bruno had to be on his toes. He appreciated Mason's talents — 'One mistake and Gary is on you like a cat' — and

Swimming, the best exercise for the whole body, is the most enjoyable part of the routine.

the two mixed it with all the power and venom of a fight for the almighty dollar.

When it was over Gary Mason knew he had earned his money. 'Frank hurts you with every shot he throws. You can't experiment or take chances because he has so much strength in every punch.' It was a situation that worried Frank. He didn't want to hurt his friends but he needed to build up his ring performance. 'It's a problem because we don't spar to hurt each other. I don't want to open up on my stablemates, that's why Terry had to pay to bring in toughnut Americans. I need a real coconut head who can take my shots and snarl back at me, otherwise I have to ease off.'

Easing off, in fact, was something trainers Jimmy Tibbs and Frank Black would have liked Frank to do. And they were getting through. Frank says now: 'I was training like

Jimmy Tibbs, Terry Lawless and Frank Black – the three men behind the throne.

If it doesn't hurt, it doesn't work – Frank shows the strain.

a lunatic because I was young, inexperienced and anxious to climb to the top as quickly as possible. I was wearing myself out and I couldn't understand why I felt so exhausted.' His trainers understood, however, and advised lighter schedules but Frank paid no heed. Instead he added extra weights to his ankles and hid them with woollen leg warmers so that his trainers would not know they were there.

But when things were at their worst he remembered some advice he had been given as an amateur: that there were too many fighters who trained their hearts out without ever stopping to practice the moves and the

tricks of the trade. 'I started taking notice of my trainers and I eased up and thought about moves and technique instead of just throwing thousands of punches. I've learned more in the last three months than I have in years.' It was just what Terry Lawless wanted: 'Years ago a mate who had been to Mexico City told me that he had watched a young fighter quietly going through moves in front of a mirror for hours, pretending to slip punches and counter, or step to one side and hook . . . much of it in slow motion. That youngster was José Napoles who went on to become one of the greatest welterweight champions. People always say he was a natural . . . don't

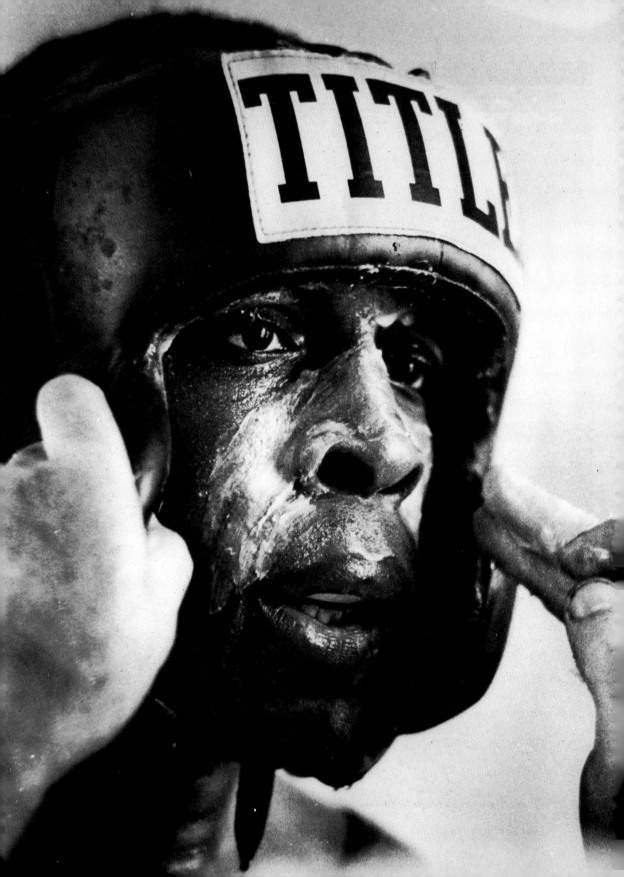

Taut muscles need to relax. Frank in a jacuzzi at Romford Baths.

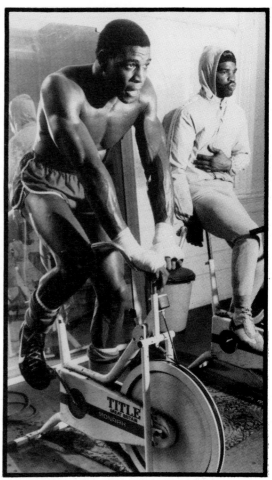

ABOVE *Going nowhere while building up the legs. A daily gym exercise.*

RIGHT *Frank loses six pounds in body weight every day – and it's hot work.*

believe it!' The Napoles lesson had been driven home and Frank spent much of his training time working on moves. He ducked and weaved and avoided imagined punches while getting his best shots square onto the invisible opponent. It was exhausting work and by the time he stopped he was six pounds lighter than when he had arrived at the gym.

With the work-out over it was back into the Granada for a 'surround-sound' drive to Romford Baths for a swim, steam bath and massage. The massage was the most important. Frank was full and praise and admiration for the skills of Rupert Doaries who kneaded and coaxed his tight and tired muscles until the whole body was relaxed and supple. The few minutes of the massage tore away the tensions of the day and Frank could go home calm enough to be the caring and

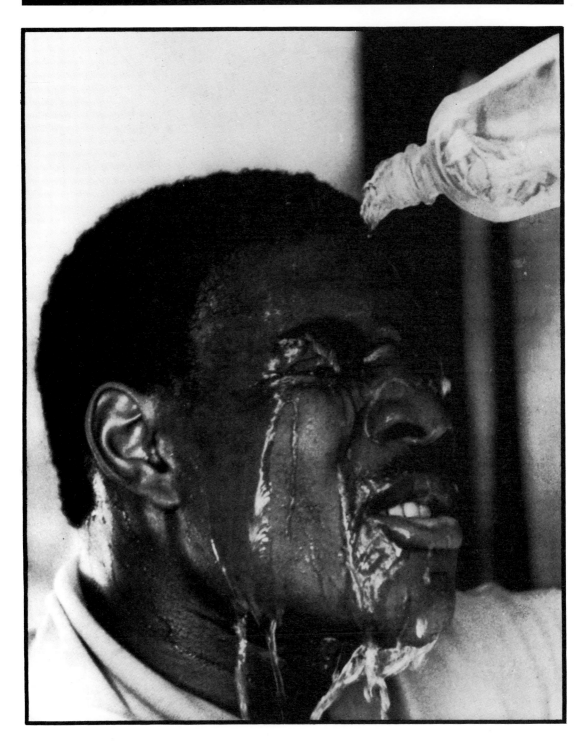

loving family man that he so enjoys being.

These days Frank still doesn't go out much in the evening and only has a small circle of friends. He is not one for nightclubs, parties and burning the candle at both ends. He remembers what happened to his boyhood hero John Conteh. 'I used to worship him and I loved to see him jump up high like he was walking on cloud nine. But look at what he's done to his life with his big bottles of champagne and so much money spent. That's not for me.' Instead Frank stays in and watches TV or boxing videos; his favourite television is 'EastEnders' and he likes science fiction movies. But whatever he does Laura is always there to make things as easy as she can for him.

My lady is 100 per cent. She met me long before I got famous so I know she didn't want me because of my success.

She's a wonderful girl. She cooks for me, looks after me and comes to all my fights without really getting much in return. I have to explain that boxing is my life. It's what I've got to do at the moment and nothing must distract me. It's hard for her, but she understands. Pressure, after all, is the most dangerous thing for me. I have to keep relaxed and cool and the last place I want pressure is at home in Essex. Laura and the kids are wonderful for keeping me happy and relaxed. I really do love their company more than anything. And when there is more time later I can enjoy lots more of it.

I know Laura doesn't like me boxing, but

Boyhood hero John Conteh, who fell from grace.

when I'm running in the morning or lifting weights I think about my other jobs . . . as a metal polisher, getting even blacker that I am, as a van driver or on a building site heaving bricks in the middle of a freezing winter . . . maybe not getting my full wage. Then I think about all the unemployed kids, old people getting beaten up for a few quid and the drugs thing. It makes me realise the need for sport of all kinds in London just to let people express themselves in some way.

And I think how, just by being a boxer, I've been able to get people to raise money for the Lady Allen Centre in Wandsworth for handicapped kids. They needed £25,000 and I never even knew what it was when I went running by it.

But Frank knows what the centre is now.

Time out for kids – and they love him.

He visits it regularly and involved himself with the progress of the children. Bill Martin of the Press Association remembers one day in particular. 'It was really quite moving to see this huge man sitting down with the children as one of them calmly painted his nose gold. He smiled all the way through it and enjoyed the fun but it must have taken him weeks to scrub the damn stuff off.'

Moments like that pay Frank back for all the sweat and pain. They are things that he could never have experienced without boxing and he wants more such experiences. Without boxing there would be no fund raising for charity, no television chat shows, no ringside banter with Harry Carpenter and no secure future for his family. 'When I get into the ring I look across at the other guy and I know that all he wants is to take my living away. I'm not going to let that happen, no way.'

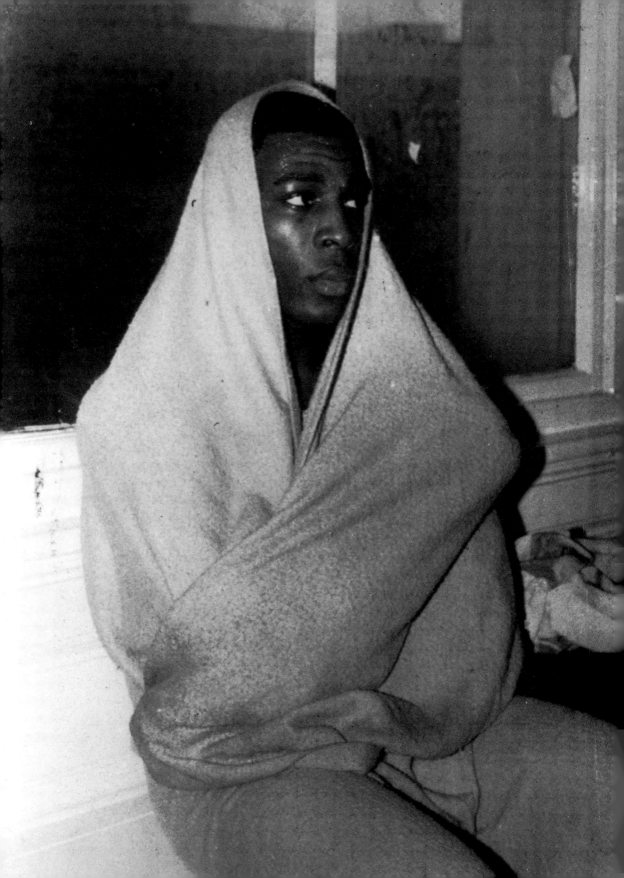

LAWLESS WINS ON POINTS

By mid 1984 everything on the boxing front seemed to be going according to plan in the Lawless gym; his fighters were doing all that he asked of them and, if it is possible for a boxing manager, he had no cares in the world. But, as always happens when things seem to be going at their smoothest, a spanner was flung deep into the most sensitive part of the Lawless operation.

A document, signed by Lawless, London promoters Mickey Duff and Mike Barrett and closed circuit TV entrepreneur Jarvis Astaire, was published in two Sunday newspapers after the Appeal Court lifted an earlier injunction against its publication. The document was an agreement between Lawless and the others to share profits from major boxing promotions at which Lawless boxers appeared. The suggestion was that the agreement created a conflict of interest for Lawless and that he was acting against the interests of the boxers in his care: a serious crime under the rules of the British Boxing Board of Control.

Under Board rules Lawless was entitled to pocket 25 per cent of his boxers' earnings on

Frank with promoter Mike Barrett (left) and Terry Lawless. With Mickey Duff and Jarvis Astaire, Lawless and Barrett form the most influential quartet in British boxing.

fights staged in the UK and 33 and a third per cent from fights staged overseas and it needed to be satisfied that the arrangements made with the other three did not restrict purses, so reducing promotion costs and creating more profits to be shared. Lawless insisted that none of his boxers had suffered because of the agreement. 'The newspapers have produced only the signatures not the document. That makes it clear there is no partnership and that we all work completely as individuals. It was purely a pool into which our earnings went, and sometimes I had to put more in from my manager's percentage than I got back from my share of the total profits.'

Terry claimed the document had been stolen from Mickey Duff's London flat as far back as 1980 and insisted that he had no fears about answering any questions about it. 'I warned my boys last Thursday that all this would be coming out in the Sunday papers and I told them that if they wished to leave, because they thought I had not done enough for them, they were free to go. I think I am the most honest man in boxing. Everything I have done has been 100 per cent for the fighters. I would back the earnings and positions of any dozen of my fighters against a dozen managed by others.' It was a powerful reply to the charges but the controversy soon began to blaze more fiercely when one of Lawless' former fighters, Sylvester Mittee, told the world on television that he was suing his former manager for failing to act in his best interests. Terry reacted as though he had been stabbed by a friend. 'It was the most wounding thing anyone could say about me. That's like saying

Frank and Nicola share a joke with neighbours at Chadwell Heath.

that every time I walk out of my house I put on a disguise and become someone else. That I'm living a lie to all the boxers in my gym. And I'm not. What I probably have been is naive.'

Something that Lawless can never be said to be, however, is naive. He is shrewd and calculating as a businessman and he would have been as aware as anyone else that, if you controlled the matchmaking, the arena and the fighters there was a far greater chance of cleaning up financially in boxing. And all he had done was to make the best of a Board of Control rule which allowed a man to manage and promote at the same time:

> I honestly don't believe I have done a thing wrong. I decided to take out the promoter's licence back in 1979 when it seemed Mickey Duff was going to be moving to the United States and leaving a

gap over here. the four of us is jus I've been looking after many years and I'm totally I see myself as opposition behalf of the fighters when we ar sing purse money. All I ever wante the best deal for them. Sometimes th have had to fight for small amounts in an effort to land a bigger payday. Jim Watt fought for only £1,000 once but it lined him up for the European title. Sylvester Mittee lost his £1,000 fight, so the plan didn't work out in his case.

It was an impassioned plea and it found a ready response in the gym where Terry's offer to release fighters who had lost confidence in him found not a single taker. Their views were summed up by Bruno who was very angry at

The agreement between
t a bit of insurance.
top fighters for
independent.
o Duff on
discus-
was

European Champion Anders Eklund, one of the few men in boxing who can make Frank look small.

the attacks on his friend and manager. 'As far as I am concerned Terry is the best manager in the world. I would be nothing without him. I don't back him 100 per cent, I back him 200 per cent.'

And a few months later the Board of Control agreed with Frank. After a six hour meeting the stewards of British boxing told the press that, after reviewing 'overwhelming evidence' from boxers under Lawless' control, that they were satisfied with purses arranged for them. Terry and the others were cleared of all charges and the Board added that, if it hadn't been for the 'active participation' of the four men 'British boxing would not be in the healthy position it is now.' Naturally Terry Lawless was delighted. 'When you are an honest man something like this throws you completely. It has been a 24 hours a day burden since it began but I never had any doubt about the result — only how long it would take.'

There is no doubt that it was a strain on Lawless and on all the boxers in his stable. For about three months British boxing was under a very black cloud and the morale of everyone in the game was lower than it had been at any time this century. But, with the Board decision, peace returned and the boxers in the Canning Town gym got down to work with increased vigour to do the very best for their manager. And in Frank Bruno's case there was a title at stake. He was to fight the Swede, Anders Eklund, for the European title.

A SWEDE FIRST COURSE

From November 1984 until October 1985 Bruno had only one fight. In April he fought former European champion Lucien Rodriguez — a fight that was over, typically, in two minutes and 39 seconds. Then he had to wait a full six months — an eternity for a boxer like Bruno who is only happy when he is in work — to meet Sweden's Anders Eklund for the European title. Eklund was to have been matched against Bruno in the spring but he complained of a hand injury and the fight was postponed. It was postponed twice more before the Wembley fans got their chance to see the title fight. In all the waiting time Bruno continued to build himself up. He never stopped working and he never stopped believing in himself — but he had something else on his mind as well as lifting the European title.

The old battle over the Burt McCarthy contract had raised it's head again. In fact the row had been rumbling on for the whole three years since the judge ruled in favour of Lawless as Frank's only manager. In that time McCarthy had been seeking damages against Bruno for not being given first option and the case was due to have a court hearing on the morning following the scheduled date of the fight against Eklund.

Carrying the burden of litigation is not the best training for a boxer after European and World crowns so the lawyers for the two sides got their heads together and, just one day before the fight, came up with an out of court settlement that was agreed by both parties. It was expensive for Frank. With costs and other expenses his total outlay was more than £100,000 but it ended a battle that had been a thorn in his side and it cleared his head for the ring battles to come. Burt McCarthy was gracious in his victory: 'What I wanted was for the world to know I was in the right. I've got nothing against Bruno personally and I wish

him good luck for the title fight. In fact, the reason I settled this was because I did not want to affect his chances.'

Not that many of the boxing writers thought Bruno was in very much danger of losing against Eklund. The big Swede had not had a very illustrious career and had surprised almost everyone in boxing when he came out of obscurity to take the European title from Norway's Steffen Tangstad in four rounds. Some thought that, perhaps, the Swede had suddenly found the right tune and that he would go from strength to strength but most felt that Bruno

---

The warm-up fight to the European Championship failed. Frank disposed of Lucien Rodriguez early in round one.

ABOVE *Journalists indicted Rodriguez for a so-called fight that was 'close to fraud'.*

RIGHT *Frank lands a well-aimed punch to the jaw of Anders Eklund . . .*

. . . And another

was in a different league. In pure physical terms they made an interesting comparison. Eklund was nearly three inches taller than Bruno and was more than half a stone heavier; he also had the advantage of an inch in reach. Bruno, on the other hand, scored hand over fist in the body development department. His biceps were a massive 17 inches against Eklund's 15 inches and his fist measured 14 inches — two and a half inches bigger than Eklund's. These are very big differences and they go a long way in explaining something of

the awesome power that Bruno packs into his body. Some university researchers, after making a study of Bruno's strength, reported that his jabs, generally reckoned to be his best punch, accelerate from zero to 200 miles an hour in just one second and that the accompanying punch is the equivalent of being hit with a ten pound hammer travelling at 20 miles an hour. Small wonder that Allan Lawrence, Frank's former headmaster, would be willing

only to be hit once — and that only if an awful lot of money was on offer.

Despite Frank's physical advantages, however, the *Mail*'s Peter Moss suggested that the long lay-off from serious competition could put him at a disadvantage against Eklund. His view was that Bruno's 'ring-rust' offered Eklund his best chance of landing a big right — his most dangerous punch. Terry Lawless heard of this criticism and was quick to fly the Bruno banner. 'You may have seen only one round in the last 11 months,' he told Moss, 'but I've seen hundreds and he has worked hard on his defence. He is now a very capable defensive boxer.' Peter Moss did think, as did all the others, that Bruno would carry the day but his fears that Frank may have defensive weaknesses were proved right towards the end of the second round.

The fight began with Bruno quicker on his feet from the bell and he went all out for a very quick win. He exploited every chance at an opening and his left jab, lightning fast, gave him immediate control over the pattern the fight would take. The 'ring-rust' was showing, however, and his big punches were a good six inches out of timing . . . he was, some said, trying too hard.

In comparison, however, Eklund looked as mobile as the NatWest Tower. He was ponderous, slow and his punches lacked any sting. Yet, somehow, near the end of round two, he found a punch that penetrated Bruno's defence. Bruno was jolted by it. For a millisecond he wasn't quite sure where he was and his legs were not doing quite what he wanted them to do. It wasn't a match winning punch and Bruno was never more than momentarily stung by it but if it had been delivered by an opponent with more class and grit than Eklund it could well have been a different story. As it was Bruno kept the initiative and, in the final minute of the third round, threw a mighty left. Eklund avoided it but ducked straight into an equally mighty right. This was followed by a left hook and a spot-on-target right and the big Swede was all but finished. He tried to hang onto Bruno but the bell went just as the staggering Eklund was separated from Bruno by the referee.

The fourth round took just ten seconds . . . ten seconds of controlled aggression. Bruno threw punches from every direction and with almost vicious power. They all landed on target. Eklund took a cut above his left eye, his mind became totally scrambled and, when his huge frame hit the canvas, there was no doubt in anyone's mind that it was all over. Frank had given the Wembley fans ten seconds of fury the like of which they had never seen before. To a man they cheered and whistled. They had a European champion and, as far as they were concerned, a possible world champion as well.

But others were not quite as ecstatic. The *Observer*'s Hugh McIlvanney, one of the more astute of the boxing writers, saw distinct danger signs. He looked at the punch that Frank took in the second round, coupled it with the near debacle against Cummings and the defeat to Bonecrusher Smith, and concluded that Frank was perhaps not quite the golden boy that others painted. McIlvanney, along with *Boxing News*' Harry Mullan, were not convinced that Bruno had the capacity to handle punches to the head, especially if they were delivered with skill and timing by genuine, hard hitting, quality heavyweights. Neither could believe that Frank could hold his own against either Pinklon Thomas, the World Boxing Council champion, or Tony Tubbs, the then WBA champion. They were gloomy thoughts but most intelligent and erudite box-

TOP LEFT *Eklund relinquishes the European Championship belt after a fourth-round Bruno knock-out.*

BOTTOM LEFT *Always gracious in victory, Frank consoles Anders Eklund and becomes the new European Champion.*

ing watchers detected the sparkle of truth in them. Most, too, would have gone along with McIlvanney when he said, 'I won't be rushing to bet on Frank against any of the leading members of the American heavy brigade.'

Frank's next fight, his last of 1985, was to have been against American Larry Alexander but, only a matter of a few days before the fight, he was sent home after the New York Athletic Commission alerted the British Boxing Board of Control that there was a suspicious looking spot on his brain scan. A new appointment had to be found in a hurry and the promoters came up with another American, Larry Frazier.

Frazier made good copy for the sports writers. He came to London by way of a two-year stretch in Soledad Maximum Security prison

Larry Frazier was a ring-in after Larry Alexander was ruled out by a suspicious brain-scan. He offered no resistance.

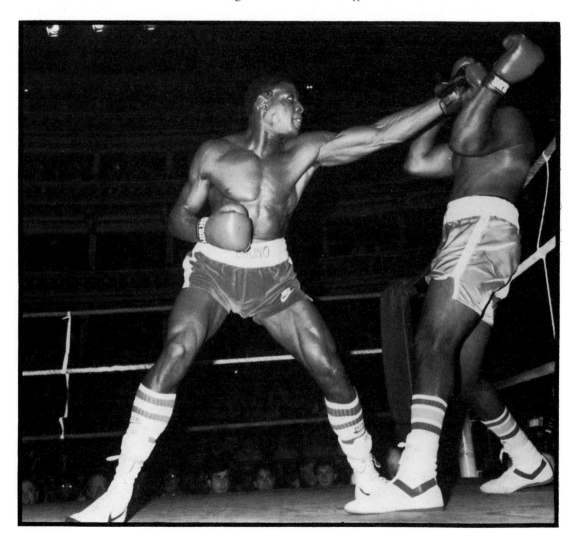

for assaulting a police officer and he rejoiced in the name Bad Boy Frazier — a title he had adopted in preference to his previous favourite . . . the Black Destroyer. But the fight should never have been allowed. Frazier was 36 years old, 12 years older than Frank. He had lost two of the three fights he had had since leaving prison and he was never going to be able to offer any serious challenge to the super-fit Bruno. It's true that Frazier had once scored a second round knock-out against former world champion Mike Weaver and had stopped Jeff Sims, the number five contender on the WBC list, in the first round. But the mauling he took now at Bruno's hands came as a surprise to no-one and left the crowd booing with displeasure.

Frazier was dispatched two minutes and fourteen seconds into the second round by a determined and almost arrogant Bruno. Frank gave every punch all he had and, when the inevitable came, stood back impassively. He appeared matter-of-fact and calm. He took the win as nothing more than his right. Frazier, on the other hand, was thankful for the end. 'I have never been hit so hard,' he said, 'If I had taken another one I may have really been badly harmed.' This from a 'hard man' who had taken punches, in and out of the ring, from some of the toughest men in the world.

It was an after-match comment that placated some. They knew Frank had not been extended but their belief that Frank was a puncher in a million was reinforced. To the British boxing public Frank was on course and running. He was a 'People's Champion' and they loved him. It was only the 'experts' who had doubts.

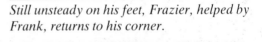

Out for the count. Frank looks concerned for Frazier after the round-two knock-out.

Still unsteady on his feet, Frazier, helped by Frank, returns to his corner.

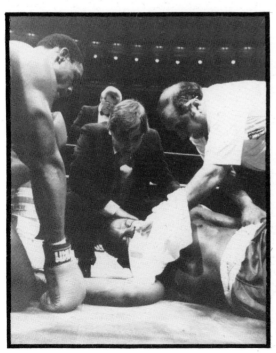

THE LAST OBSTACLE

The demolition job on Eklund and the capture of the European Championship gave rise to gleeful high spirits in the Lawless camp but Terry's gut feeling was that he would like to give Frank another year to develop before lining up a title shot. He knew that Frank was still very much an apprentice in the top heavyweight league but he also knew, too well, the intensity of Bruno's ambition. He was going to have to let Frank fight anyone. Terry said at the time:

> It has come to the stage when it would be difficult to turn down a world title fight and tell Frank I had done so. But I would still only take it if there was enough money to set him up for life. Frank is off the leash but the money must be right. If it is not we will wait. I'm in no rush, I see him as improving day by day in the gym. It's possible he could be fighting for the world title within a year but nobody is going to hustle me.'

Nevertheless match-maker Mickey Duff set off almost immediately for the States with priority number one a 'meaningful fight for Bruno' — and the obvious choice was former champion and number one contender Gerrie Coetzee of South Africa. Coetzee was the main contender despite having been knocked out by Greg Page a year before and many felt he would not risk his heir-to-the-throne position unless the financial carrot was very large indeed.

In America at this time top promoter Don King was planning a series of fights to find the genuine world heavyweight champion from all three of the competing boxing authorities. He had made his plans and negotiations were reasonably advanced when Duff brought Bruno into the picture as an interloper — but there was an ace up Mickey Duff's sleeve:

King had put the whole thing together, and he had everybody. He didn't have to bother about Coetzee because he was a South African who everybody could refuse to fight for political reasons. Don was busy at that time fighting a court case for tax evasion and, while all that was going on,, I made the Bruno and Coetzee fight and got the WBA to recognise it as a final eliminator to decide the number one contender. Therefore if Bruno was to win this fight nobody could refuse to fight him. He is not South African, just a black boxer that happened to be a genuine challenger.'

In effect, what Mickey Duff had done was to offer Frank a possibility of a shortcut to a championship bout. Coetzee was the top contender but no one wanted to fight him. If

Lawless, Bruno and Duff at the announcement of the final eliminator.

Bruno did, and beat him, he would become the top contender himself. It was a chance too good to miss.

But when the announcement of the fight was made there were howls of protest from the anti-Apartheid lobby, and from some eminent people in boxing itself. Frank was surprised, for instance, to find that his friend, former world light-middleweight champion Maurice Hope, had come out against the fight. A statement issued on behalf of Hope and another former world champion, John Conteh, said: 'We make an earnest appeal for you to call off the fight. The only benefactor of this fight will be Apartheid.'

The statement may have been a surprise to Bruno, it was even more of a surprise to Hope, who said:

> 'I'm being used. I'm being made to look a fool. I had a phone call inviting me to a dinner and asking me how I felt about the Bruno–Coetzee fight. If it had been me I would not have fought a South African but that's only a personal opinion. There is no way I would try to talk Frank out of it and I don't want to be part of any campaign. It is his decision. Fighting a South African could mean problems for him later. It could result in him being banned from some countries and not accepted in some sections of this country but Frank has to make the final decision himself.'

John Conteh, too, had second thoughts after advising Bruno not to support South Africa's 'fascist regime'. 'When I put my name to that letter to Frank I had really thought about it, I didn't rush at it. But in retrospect I think I was wrong. It was me trying to impose my will on someone else, which is precisely the thing I was against in the first place.' Conteh had had some experience of the South African connection

himself. When he was world champion he was offered two fights with huge purses. They were to be against Pierre Fourie and Victor Galindez but they were South African promotions and the fights were to be staged in South Africa. Conteh turned them both down. 'For a non-white to go down there and earn money was just not possible for me but Frank must check his own conscience and come to his own decision.'

Although Hope and Conteh publicly withdrew from the organised campaign against the fight some others did not. Many leading figures in the boxing establishment remained opposed to the fight but Frank and Terry Lawless were determined from the start to go ahead with it. They both knew how important it was for Frank's future career and they were both unimpressed by the anti-Apartheid arguments. Coetzee had made many statements critical of his country's regime and it was well known that his main sparring partner and friend was a black man he had helped raise from the bottom of the system. The Lawless camp saw these as the actions of a man of principle and saw the fight as a bout against a man, not the whole South African system.

Others agreed with them. Jim Watt, who boxed in South Africa before becoming world lightweight champion, put Bruno's case in a nutshell. 'If Bruno doesn't go through with the fight then in two years' time the people who persuaded him to pull out will have forgotten his name. If he does go through with it, though, he can make a million pounds and give his family security for life. He's a professional; that's what he's supposed to do.'

And the public, too, were largely behind the fight because the bookmakers had made Frank the favourite — against the advice of many of the boxing pundits. Coetzee's reputation with boxing fans and the bookies was based largely on his last two fights — which had been far from impressive — but the boxing writers and

Coetzee's trainer Jack McCoy insisted it was necessary to look further back than that. McCoy agreed with the criticism about Coetzee's two previous fights but added: 'He wasn't right for those fights. Against Page his right hand, that had those fifteen operations, was giving trouble and they put five different shots

---

South African Gerrie Coetzee poses with Frank and the Mexican gloves he insisted on for the fight. Frank had wanted British gloves.

into him to kill the pain. He was so sedated that he said before the fight "I don't feel nervous at all." And when he fought Quick Tillis he was not himself. He had had flu and his mother had died a little before.' He insisted that for the Bruno fight Coetzee was spot on and he loudly proclaimed his belief that the South African would knock Frank out in the early rounds.

Doug Bidwell, the manager of Glen McCrory, a heavyweight who was sparring

Mean and moody, but the
perfect gentleman.
Meet Frank Bruno MBE,
the WBC Heavyweight
Champion of the World.

The Bruno entourage, including Nigel Benn. enters Wembley stadium before the McCall fight.

Frank, a study of focus and determination, exchanges blows with Oliver McCall.

Take that. Bruno troubles McCall with a powerful left hook.

Bruno continues his tremendous onslaught as he tries to breech McCall's desperate defences.

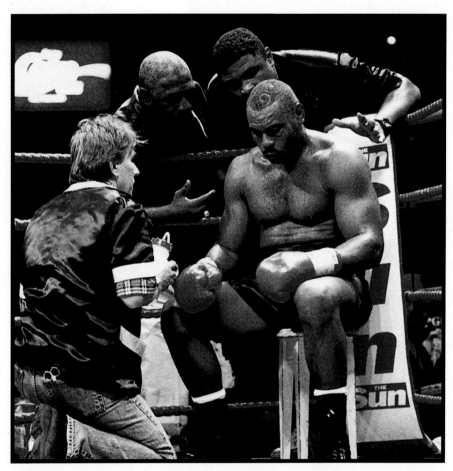

Words of wisdom for Oliver McCall. It was now or never for the defending champion. The choice was simple, knock out Bruno, or surrender the WBC crown to the Englishman.

The realisation of a life-long dream.
Frank accepts the acclaim of an ecstatic crowd.

He's finally done it. The crowd rushes into the ring to share their joy with Big Frank.

The Bruno family celebrate the famous victory.
From left to right, daughter Nicola,
Frank and wife Laura.

*The pride of England. Daughter
Rachel proudly holds Dad's
WBC belt aloft.*

with Coetzee in the build-up to the fight, agreed with McCoy. 'I can't see Bruno beating Coetzee except on cuts, and he does cut. Coetzee is very well and fit. He is heavy but I was surprised to see how light he is on his feet. He has got a very good left hook and a very fast right hand and good body moves. I want Bruno

Even at the weigh-in Frank looked the fitter but, surprisingly, some boxing writers made him the underdog.

to win because it will do British boxing good but, really, Coetzee looks too good. I cannot understand the bookmakers making Bruno the favourite. I think Coetzee will surprise everyone and end the fight early.'

On paper, certainly, Coetzee looked a class above Bruno — he had been in with some of the toughest men in the game. He had knocked out Leon Spinks in one, he was knocked out by Mike Weaver in 13 rounds but not before having the American virtually beaten and out

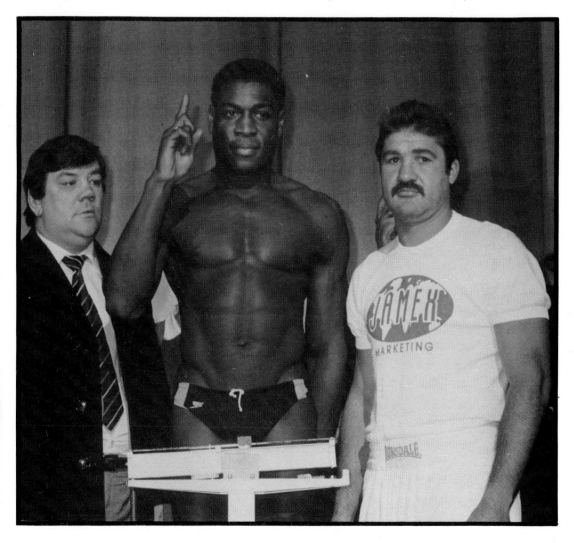

on his feet in the eighth. He lost to Renaldo Snipes on a controversial split decision after flooring the American twice and he drew with Pinklon Thomas in 1983 before taking the title from Dokes. The general feeling was that, with all that experience, he must be able to land a couple of his big punches and Bruno was known to have a vulnerable chin. Memories of Jumbo Cummings and Bonecrusher Smith came flooding back and the experts saw Coetzee as the man capable of ending Frank's championship hopes. They also knew how badly Coetzee wanted to win the fight. He wanted to go and live in America and he wanted to be part of King's tournament to find an undisputed world champion. Bruno stood in his way for both and many of boxing's most intelligent students felt that Coetzee's experience, plus his strong incentive, would succeed in brushing the Bruno opposition aside.

But when the March 4 fight date came around Bruno got into the ring as ever in magnificent shape and Coetzee, patently, did not. Frank oozed confidence, his manner told the crowd that he expected to win and that he was already the top contender for the title. Coetzee, on the other hand, had obviously gone to seed. He was more than heavy, he was fat. Even pulling up his shorts to cover most of his midriff could not hide the blubber of his belly. If it wasn't for the fact that, on paper, Coetzee looked the good bet it would have been a 'no-contest'. Nobody, after once having seen both fighters in the ring, could have been in any doubt that Bruno would win.

And win he did in the most impressive of manners. From the beginning Frank was on the attack. He drove his target around the ring with a series of jabs, each of which brimmed over with self-confidence. Coetzee, having felt the sting of the quick-fire jabs, retreated but Bruno, shifting his weight nicely, got in a right to the head that sent Coetzee sprawling. The ex-champion got up after three but he was cut

on the cheek and took the rest of the eight count to get his breath. When the fight resumed Bruno was relentless. He hammered in jolting rights and, after just 110 seconds of battle, landed another right that had Coetzee down and half out of the ring. It was an ignominious end for a former world champion. Gerrie Coetzee had given much to boxing but Bruno's right signalled the end of his career. You don't come back from hammerings like that.

With Bruno's final punch the crowd went wild with delight. The enemy was on the floor and a British boy was knocking on the door of the world championship. It made for a heady night.

After the fight Frank held court in a small Wembley room, full of pride in what he had done, and without even raising a sweat. He jabbered away, thanking everyone he could think of, from God and Terry Lawless down to his trainers and his mother — 'I don't wanna sound like Barry McGuigan or nothing but I've got a whole lot of thanking to do — know what I mean'. The alcoholic combination of adrenalin and victory had Frank gushing with words — some of which he may later have regretted. 'I went to see Gerrie Coetzee in his dressing room and I said, "Gerrie, I'm really sorry to disgrace you in front of your wife and children and all those people," — I just wanted him to know, like.' Kenneth Clarke, Cabinet Minister and avid boxing fan who was in that select audience, winced at the word 'disgrace'. 'Dear me,' said the then Postmaster General, 'He's certainly not a politician, is he?'

Politician he may not have been but Frank Bruno had to take just as many thunderbolts as any politician after the fight. Journalists and armchair experts who, before the fight, had been saying that Coetzee should be considered the marginal favourite now blasted the former champion for not being a serious opponent and for not treating the fight seriously. And Lawless got his share of stick for only putting Frank up against 'bums and no-hopers'. It was criticism that Frank had heard many times before — and it always made him see red:

> People say I just knock over bums, but bums don't go in the ring. They stay in pubs, they stay out in the street and sleep in parks. Bums don't go in the ring because boxing isn't a game like that. You have to think about it and plan your moves. You plan very carefully. One little slip and you could be knocked out. That's why boxers work on concentration, fitness development and stamina. If a man is as strong as you are and has a strong chin you have to suss him out — weaken him with belly shots and uppercuts. You've got to shock him, jerk him, make him tense and wear him down. Sometimes you fake that you're tired so that the man comes in, gets mad, and uses up all his energy. It's a very powerful chess game . . . not the sort of thing for bums at all.

Certainly in Coetzee's case there was no question. His connections believed their man would win and had money on the result. In the traditional 'eye-balling' session before the fight

Shorts pulled high to cover his paunch, Coetzee was never any match for Frank.

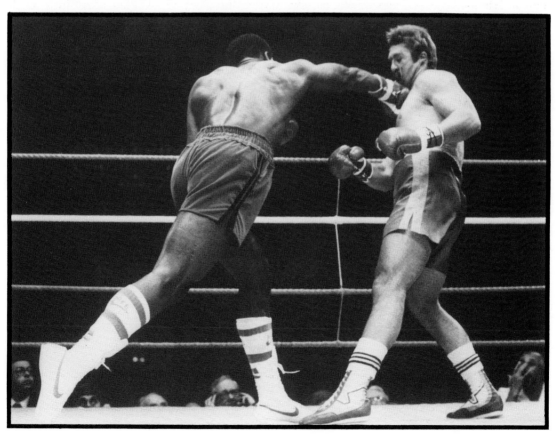

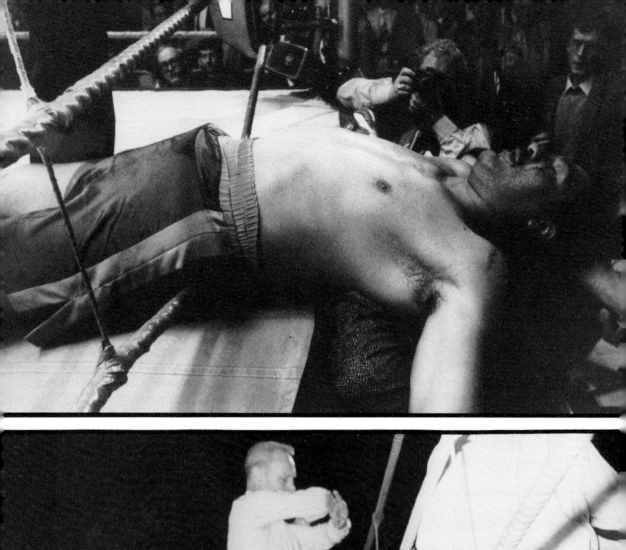

began Coetzee would have to have been a better actor than Paul Newman to fake his obviously aggressive intent. The important thing — something overlooked by most people — was that Frank showed the maturity not to let the pre-fight dramatics unnerve him. He was not intimidated by Coetzee in the slightest.

He tried to give me the eyeball but I just stared back. I knew he had to have a sledgehammer to knock me out. I had the sledgehammer. No one else has ever done what I did to Gerrie. Ever. I felt so relaxed, I felt like a baboon, so loose, so easy, so unconcerned. I might have been just a little bit nervous thinking he would come faster at me. But, oh man, the power I felt in my hands. Gerrie had said all week that I was a manufactured fighter. He said I came from Tesco's, but as he fell he looked at me for a split second and he seemed to be saying, 'My God, where's this fellow learned to punch like that.'

I really think I might be the best now — okay, I don't want to get all flash and I know I'm not the most stylish. I'm no fancy lollipop boxer dancing round like a girl — like Pinklon Thomas and that lot. I'm not stylish but I'm the fittest and strongest — I really reckon that.

Others reckoned it too. His blink-of-the-eye destruction of Coetzee had echoed around the world. The once over-aggressive little boy of Wandsworth was saying to the top clique in the American heavy brigade, 'Hey, you're in my place.' They knew they couldn't avoid him, that sooner or later they would have to meet the Limey interloper.

LEFT *The end of the farcical fight and a fine career. Bruno is now the number one contender.*

Terry Lawless, as usual ever-conscious of his fighter's best interests, would have been quite happy to wait as long as possible before putting Frank up against the Americans, but the pressure was on. Big money was at stake, for the promoters even more than Frank, and Mickey Duff and Frank Barrett immediately began talking with Don King about getting Frank a title shot; but the problem was deciding who was the WBA heavyweight champion.

'Terrible' Tim Witherspoon had overcome title-holder Tony Tubbs in a match in the states but the post-fight blood-test had revealed traces of marijuana in Witherspoon. At first the conjecture was that Witherspoon would be stripped of the title and have to re-fight Tubbs before Bruno could get a shot. This was not favoured by Duff and Barrett because they wanted to stage Britain's biggest heavyweight contest for years at Wembley — and that meant getting Witherspoon first. Protracted negotiations were held until Mickey Duff was able to say: 'We have agreed terms with Bruno, we have agreed terms with Witherspoon, who is managed by Don King, we have agreed terms with Tony Tubbs and Tony Tubbs has agreed the terms to stand aside. Now the problem is what to do in the event of a Bruno win. Tubbs has to be the next fight and we have to agree the terms and the venue for that — and it all has to fit into Don King's plans. King needs the winner to be available for the whole of the series . . . and there are many things to be sorted out yet.'

That was in May 1986 — just two months before the tentative date for the Wembley fight of July 19. It seemed the fight was on, there were one or two things still to sort out but Duff, Barrett and King were experienced promoters and they had been through it all before. There seemed no reason why the fight shouldn't go ahead as planned. But those who were counting their chickens were counting without considering the horny question of tele-

Terrible Tim Witherspoon, knocked down only once, and then as an amateur, the obstacle to the World Heavyweight crown.

Wembley, the scene of England's World Cup success and the venue for Bruno's lifetime goal – a home ground advantage?

vision. Duff and Barrett always worked with the BBC but ITV had sent it's Head of Sport to Las Vegas and concluded a deal with Don King for exclusive coverage of the whole championship series. The Duff camp were incensed and the fight looked doomed, only Terry Lawless had a smile on his face. He knew that if the fight didn't go ahead at Wembley, Tubbs and Witherspoon would have to re-fight in America with Bruno having an automatic shot at the winner within 90 days. Terry knew that Frank would benefit every day from gym work and the longer the camp waited the better Bruno's chances were. Frank wanted to fight in front of a home crowd and give them the championship

they so badly wanted but if he had to win it in the States then defend it in the UK, so be it.

The TV wrangle went on and on and became quite bitter. It seemed there was no solution in sight but Frank Barrett came up with one. There would be no TV at the Wembley fight. It would go ahead as planned on July 19 and it would be filmed for later screening in cinemas around the country. Not a perfect solution but a solution nevertheless. The fight was to go on: Frank Bruno of England was to meet Tim Witherspoon of America for the World Boxing Association's Heavyweight Championship of the World. Frank's moment had come at last.

BACK TO SQUARE ONE

The person least concerned with all the wheeling and dealing over television rights for the championship fight with Witherspoon was Terry Lawless. In fact he would not have objected if the problems had become deadlocked. Terry was fighting a losing battle in trying to restrain an eager Frank but he knew that the longer Bruno waited the better his chances would be and Lawless, always keen to give his fighters the best possible chance, wanted that breathing space.

> If the fight does not come off Witherspoon will meet Tony Tubbs for the WBA title and the WBA have ordered that the winner must meet Bruno within 90 days. We can wait that 90 day period, or longer if necessary. It would do Bruno no harm. Since he won the final eliminator I have watched him develop until he has become a giant in every way. He handles people and situations superbly now. He is involved almost every day of the week in some project or other outside boxing but he never neglects training. Nobody has to remind him how important it is.

Lawless knew that at 24, and without the bruising American street fighting tradition behind him, Frank was the baby of the big leagues. If he had been in total control of all phases of promotion and management there is little doubt he would have given his friend another eighteen months or two years before he shot for the title but Frank was an irresistible force. He was confident, strong and almost desperately committed to winning a world heavyweight crown for Britain. Terry didn't have a hope in a current that strong.

As it was the TV fiasco resolved itself. The fight would be staged at 1.00 am so that it could go out live on Home Box Office cable TV on the eastern seaboard of the States. British TV would record the fight and screen it the following day. The only thing left to decide was which of the UK TV networks would screen the fight first and this was solved in the manner of gentlemen — by the toss of a coin. ITV would screen the fight at 9.30 the following morning and BBC would screen it on its Sunday evening programmes. It was the last obstacle out of the way. The green light was on for the fight to go ahead and conditions were ripe for the traditional 'hype' war between the rival camps to begin.

Not that Bruno is a natural for the 'Ah'm gonna moider dat bum' game. He is far too nice, too sensitive to the feelings of others and too honest with himself to overstep the mark in pre-fight banter. He was going to put his trust in God and he would give it his 'very best shot'. His view was that he had trained hard for the fight and that if he wasn't ready he never would be. It was heart-warming, modest stuff and it attracted thousands more fans to his camp and, paradoxically, added that much more pressure to his massive shoulders when the fight finally came around.

Even at the first pre-fight Press conference Frank limited his comments to reiterating his view that Witherspoon was a 'great champion' but added that he thought he would win because of the champion's frenetic social lifestyle.

On the other hand Witherspoon, who had arrived in England with a small army of minders that included, in the last fortnight before the fight, a sad shadow of a man who used to rejoice in the name of Mohammed Ali, was full of hot air and bombast. What he wasn't going

---

The fight is on, and Frank starts well in his bid for the World Heavyweight crown.

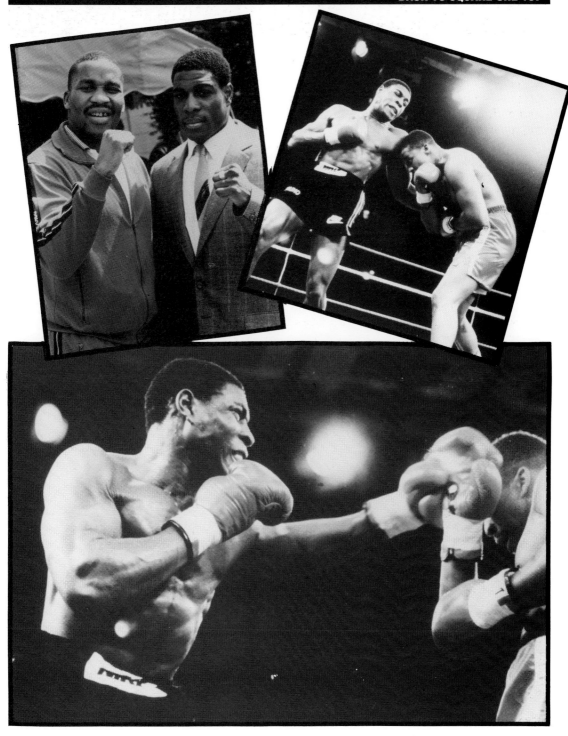

to do to Frank was nobody's business. A knockout in the seventh round seemed to be his favourite prediction. Frank was good, he conceded, but he was British and no British boxer ever stood a chance against an American — QED.

Once the war of pre-fight publicity words began the Press, so adept at making Mount Everests out of insignificant facial pimples, began to take over. They didn't need the rival camps actually to say anything, they could whip it along quite happily themselves, thank you. Bruno was too tense and worried. He was hiding himself away in the Lawless gym — away from the stares of Press and public — because he was uptight and he didn't want this conveyed to the Witherspoon camp. Naturally

this was denied by Terry Lawless. He told the Press that Frank was being cossetted away because his training was very important and it was felt that having swarms of people around every day in the gym would distract him from the job in hand. It was a reasonable explanation, especially given the fact that Frank was such a young and inexperienced challenger, but the tabloid Press continued with the 'tense and worried' Bruno theme.

Witherspoon, on the other hand, was not taking his training seriously. He was, said banner headlines, overweight and sloppy. He was more interested in having a good time than training and he was likely to get into the ring as

Witherspoon stages his comeback . . .

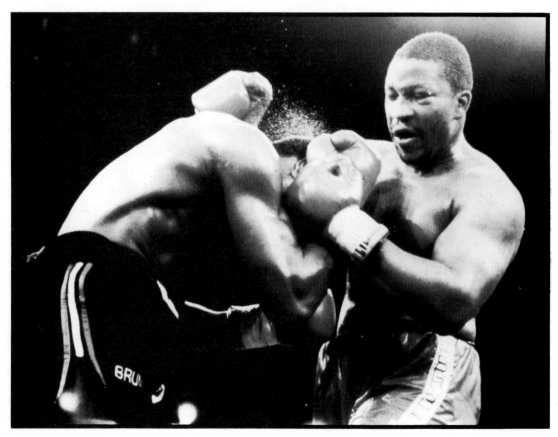

unprepared as Coetzee. If he did, they said, Frank would have no trouble knocking him out.

It was speculation that resulted in Frank going into the fight favourite and it was a disservice. Frank had enough to carry without the added burden of favouritism and the Press, many of whom, it seems, would have difficulty telling a boxing boot from a ski boot, have to take some of the blame for Frank trying too hard, too early, on the night.

What Frank needed was sympathetic and realistic support. He was getting it from the public — over 4,000 letters a week were pouring through his letter box — but he needed

. . . and the sparks are flying.

more and it came, surprisingly, from his mother. Lynette had always said she would never go to see her son fight. She loathed boxing and she couldn't bear the prospect of seeing her son hurt but, for this major occasion, she relented and agreed to watch Frank at Wembley. He was overjoyed. He was proud of what he did and deeply honoured to be doing the job for his country. So much so that his fondest wish was for his mother and family to be there to see him perform:

My Mum hasn't seen me fight since I was in my cot. Usually, when I fight, she is in the toilet with her Bible, praying. In the past she has always said no to my pleas that she should come and, even this time,

it took her a week to make up her mind. I'm thrilled she has agreed to be there and it will make me all the more determined — if that's possible.

Unfortunately it takes more than simple determination to win fights and, on the night, his determination blinded him; he could hardly see the wood for the trees. Buoyed by a tidal wave of crowd support — over 40,000 people who, with the exception of a few Witherspoon followers and a handful of National Front lunatics who hissed their obscene, mindless hatred, cheered for him to a man — Frank could not help but feel the weight of his ambition and his responsibility as he came into the ring. As

usual he looked fantastic and his body was in perfect shape. Witherspoon was the opposite. At 16 stone 10 pounds he was half a stone heavier than Frank and about three quarters of a stone over what most observers considered his best fighting weight. His counter to the criticism of his well-padded midriff was that he needed a little bulk there to absorb the power of Frank's mighty punches. Hindsight suggests there may well be more than a grain of truth in this.

For the first six rounds Frank gave his fans everything they could have wanted except a knockout. He moved well, he boxed well, he put together combinations and he answered many critics by taking some of Witherspoon's

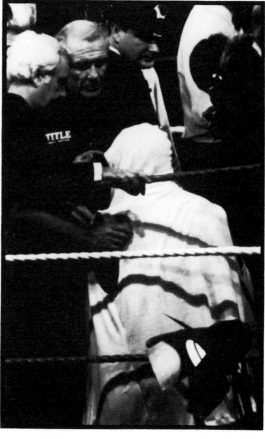

best shots without obvious discomfort. In those six rounds there was genuine hope that Britain could end the night with a heavyweight champion. But whereas Witherspoon was relaxed and pacing himself, Bruno had his brow permanently furrowed with concentration. He was thinking himself out of being natural and he was burning up his nervous energy as fast as a Grand Prix car burns petrol. It took its toll.

Round seven was marginal but rounds eight, nine and ten went easily to Witherspoon. It was as though Frank had tried all his tricks and plans and had nothing left — and even when he did put something together the thinking process behind it meant it was invariably a few milliseconds off perfect timing. In addition Witherspoon was taking the best of what Frank had to offer without blinking an eye. There can be no doubt that he was being hurt but it didn't stop him. He launched attack after attack with his whole body hurtling forward and with both arms swinging haymaking punches. Most of them failed to connect but Frank could not counter these charges and it became obvious that the end was not too far away.

In the eleventh Frank made a final, last-ditch attempt and he landed two of his best punches of the night but, as he was doing so, Witherspoon landed two even better ones. Frank was rocked and a more experienced fighter would have gone down and taken a compulsory eight count to get himself together. But Frank was thinking only about winning and he went in again at Witherspoon like a kamikaze pilot.

The end was seconds away. Completely disorientated and with his guard around his waist Frank was an open target and Witherspoon mercilessly pounded him — even landing two completely unnecessary blows when Frank was already down. At that moment the bell for the end of the round went but the referee had already stopped it and Terry Lawless had sensibly thrown in the towel from the Bruno corner.

It was the end of a great dream but the big man from Wandsworth had done us proud. He had shown guts aplenty and he had surprised the American camp with the ferocity of his challenge. Tim Witherspoon was unstinting in his praise:

> I always thought he wouldn't be a pushover. It was a tough fight and he hurt me, hurt me more than I've been hurt before. Sure, he was beaten tonight but he shouldn't give up. He is a good fighter and maybe someday he can be world champion.

The sentiment was echoed by American promoter Don King: 'This was the night Bruno the boy became the man. He came of age in that ring and I can see him getting another shot at the title in about 18 months. He deserves it'.

The end of a dream for a dazed Frank Bruno. The crown has slipped through his fingers and he is back under wraps — until next time.

COMING BACK FROM THE DEAD

After Witherspoon Frank weathered a storm of Fleet Street flak. The same Press that had been hyping him up before the fight now called him mediocre and intimated that they had always known he wouldn't be able to stand up to a 'real' opponent.

Even his former trainer Jimmy Tibbs was more than just a little critical.

> Frank is very determined and willing, and works hard at anything he's shown, but he has no natural ability. He's very strong but stiffens up in the ring and relies too much on his jab. Mobile opponents confuse him . . . and there's no instinct for holding and hanging on when he gets hurt. I wanted Lawless to bring in some tough sparring partners but he wasn't keen. You can over-protect fighters.

But in March 1987 Frank was matched against a man who was certainly no has-been and who could legitimately be called a contender. That man was James 'Quick' Tillis. Tillis arrived with a fight CV that could be matched by no other heavyweight in the world at that time: he had gone the full distance against Mike Tyson. He had also taken the former champion Mike Weaver 15 rounds in an attempt to wrest the WBA heavyweight title from him.

Terry Lawless was convinced that Tillis would be a tough challenge for Bruno and that a win would re-establish Frank as a force in the heavyweight division.

> I know Tillis very well. Frank, Tillis and Tyson have all been in the same gym together, when they trained in the United States a few years ago. At the time Tillis was probably the leading heavyweight contender. He is a very

smart guy and knows his way around, and probably gave Tyson his toughest fight last year. If I remember rightly he was ahead after eight rounds before Tyson put in a storming finish.

Media interest was intense before the Wembley fight. Lawless and Bruno were not talking about a possible match with Tyson but the Press knew that a Bruno win would almost certainly lead to a multi-million dollar Anglo-American confrontation, a belief heightened by the fact that Tyson was in England for the fight, apparently intent on sizing up Frank as a possible opponent.

In the event Frank punched his way back not only to a secure position in the heavyweight division top ten but also into the hearts of the win-starved British boxing public. It was eight months since the Witherspoon defeat but Frank showed no ring-rust. In the opening rounds he kept his cool as the experienced Tillis held and spoiled in an open attempt to force Bruno out of his stride. By the fifth, Frank was streets ahead on points and he unleashed a flurry of rapid-fire blows which had Tillis reeling and struggling back to his corner with a left eyebrow cut. Blood poured down his face and onto the white of his shorts. Referee John Coyle had no option but to stop the contest.

It was a very professional performance by Bruno — and it was impressive enough to have many of the boxing writers questioning their earlier reservations about him. Even

Hands aloft, Bruno is back in business after an impressive performance against James Tillis. The referee stopped the fight at the end of the fifth round, with blood pouring from Tillis's left eyebrow.

Tyson was impressed by what he saw. 'Frank did a tremendous job,' he said, 'It was difficult for him at the start because Tillis is very experienced, but he kept working at it until, finally, he got through. He will make a good opponent for me and I look forward to fighting him.'

Bruno himself was also delighted by his performance.

> It ain't easy fighting someone like that and I'm pleased about the way I did it. He was supposed to be gone, shot, but he was quick and very experienced and, let's face it, there was a hell of a lot of pressure on me out there . . . quite frankly, I couldn't have walked in here to speak to you people if I had lost. But I didn't, I won, and, after all that has happened to me recently, I'm encouraged and I am looking forward to meeting Mike Tyson.

Everyone agreed, some with confidence but most with lingering reservations, that Frank was on his way. But his star was brought crashing down two months later with an appallingly one-sided, 59-second annihilation of overweight and incompetent American Chuck Gardner at Cannes in France.

The fight could only take place in Europe as the British Boxing Board of Control had refused Gardner a licence to fight in the UK — and rightly so: it was the equivalent of the New Zealand All Blacks playing an English schoolboy side, a no-contest. Indeed, it so shocked and angered the millions of TV boxing fans that former Sports Minister Denis Howell called for a government investigation after he was told that no-hoper Gardner had a twisted ankle and was amazed to find himself in the same ring as Bruno. 'It all suggests that Gardner should never have been fighting,' the Labour MP said as he urged Sports Minister

Colin Moynihan, a former steward with the British Boxing Board of Control, to probe the matter.

Gardner confessed that he had only been told about the fight 25 days before it was due to take place. He said he had twisted his ankle working on a building site and was surprised to get the opportunity to fight Bruno who, his manager had admitted, was 2,000–1 on. But the American was unrepentant about taking the fight. 'I didn't call anyone asking to be in there with Bruno — they came begging for me to take the fight. I couldn't believe it, he's in a different class to me. But I also couldn't believe how much money I was going to get. They promised me £3,000, which would have paid a few of my bills, but I haven't seen a cent. The whole thing has been a nightmare and now I'm even further in debt.'

However, Lawless, prior to the fight, refused to make any excuses for setting up the bout.

> We're not beating drums or anything about the fight, that's why it makes me sick when people criticise Frank's opponent. Frank is not even top of the bill, it's a down-the-bill fight — it's just a job. Remember, too, that this is only the second fight since the battle with Witherspoon, which was the most punishing night of his life. Yet Frank gets murdered because we take a fight like this. It's not as if we were claiming that a win over Gardner makes him ready for Mike Tyson. He can't be fighting eight or nine people in the top 10 all the time. You study the record of

A team effort: Frank Bruno, with Terry Lawless (left) and George Francis (right), prepares to meet Joe Bugner in the fight that boxing fans had always wanted to see but many thought would never happen.

most of the top heavyweights in the world and they all have their share of fights against opponents very few people have heard of. It's just a way of keeping Frank active. He is very keen for action and is always pestering to be in on every show.

Boxing Board of Control General Secretary John Morris said the Board had no control over a contest in Cannes but admitted that the British authorities should have expressed their concerns more vigorously. As a postscript to the Cannes fiasco, promoter

Mike Barrett ended his association with Terry Lawless, Mickey Duff and Jarvis Astaire. 'It was ludicrous,' he said. 'The public were simply not getting value for money.'

There can be little doubt that both Bruno and his management were stung by the ferocity of the criticism that followed the Gardner debacle, but it seemed that they had

Joe Bugner covers up as Frank moves in with a barrage of punches. Bruno stopped the new Australian Bugner in eight rounds, much to the delight of a partisan crowd at White Hart Lane.

not learned a lesson from it as they followed up, two months later, with another hopeless mismatch, this time against Reggie Gross at Marbella in Spain. Gross was no more credible an opponent than Gardner, but Frank used the fight as a sparring session and the referee did not feel compelled to stop the bout until round eight. It was just an opportunity to get more ring experience: as Terry Lawless would have said, just part of the job.

Gross was, however, the last of Bruno's embarrassments for some time as his next fight, at White Hart Lane, Tottenham, in October 1987, was the one that most British boxing fans wanted to see — Bruno versus the Mighty Mouth himself, Joe Bugner. Arranging this bout was something of a coup for snooker promoter Barry Hearn, who conducted all the negotiations with former champion new Australian Bugner. It was predicted that the fight would generate £2,000,000 and the Press, not to mention the bookmakers, had a field day.

Bogus 'hatreds' were contrived between the two fighters and Bugner contributed joyfully to the circus atmosphere with some pre-fight crowing that would have been worthy of Mohammed Ali at his best.

The guy will go for sure. A lot of right-handers will be thrown out there. One of them will connect and that will be enough. I've been after Bruno for six years. It annoyed me when he said I was chicken about the fight . . . well, you tell him the chicken has come home to roost. It won't be me who gets hit. I'm a crafty old dog. Henry Cooper said I have the heart of a pea. These old fighters should keep quiet. Henry should stick to golf. His record does not compare to mine. A lot of people say I can't punch, but I say ask the 38 people I have knocked out.

Bruno's reaction to all this was to smile and let it ride. He wasn't playing the prediction game but he knew that hype puts bums on seats. 'I say, keep going, Joe my son. The more you go on rabbiting the more tickets you will sell and the richer I will be.' And that is exactly how it turned out. Mr Nice Guy Bruno whipped the old bogeyman from the first bell and the referee put an end to it in round eight. It was a drubbing, a very professional drubbing, and the crowd of 30,000 loved every second.

From the moment Bugner appeared, draped in the Australian flag (he had shrewdly secured Australian TV rights for himself in the fight negotiations), the crowd was baying for his blood. Every time Bruno landed a punch they screamed their delight and, when Frank stepped it up a gear and despatched Bugner with a viciousness that few had seen in him before, they were positively delirious.

It was the end of Bugner: the man who had specialised in come-backs announced his final retirement immediately after the fight, which established Bruno as the number one contender for Mike Tyson's WBC title. Suddenly the boy from Wandsworth was above Michael Spinks, Pinklon Thomas, Trevor Berbick and Tyrell Biggs in the rankings and the fight Bruno had set his heart on was no longer just a dream, it was mandatory.

After the announcement of the Bruno–Tyson clash, the recently beaten Joe Bugner, never one to leave out his two cents'-worth, surprisingly backed Bruno to beat Iron Mike. 'Tyson is very limited,' he insisted. 'His style of fighting is fine behind pubs, but he lacks finesse. He is crude, unsophisticated and has only a limited amount of ability. Bruno's punch could easily upset Tyson. He certainly punched me harder than I thought he could. I think Bruno has every chance.'

In typical Bugner style, it was the kiss of death.

THE IRON MIKE SHOWDOWN

Iron Mike Tyson's brutish image softened considerably when he talked about Frank Bruno. The two had met several times. They had trained and sparred in the same gym and Tyson had spent some time with Bruno when he came to England to see him fight James Tillis. And no one doubted that Tyson harboured genuine affection for Frank, as he told almost anyone who would listen.

I think Frank is a really great guy. He is so well mannered and so respectful; whenever we've met I've never heard him bad-mouth anyone. I know he is no hell-raiser and that he is the dedicated family man. He is always telling me about his two lovely daughters. There is no way I would want to hurt him or to bust him up. That's why, for the sake of his family as well as himself, I will take him out in the opening round. He knows I always try to get a fight over as quickly as possible — just as he does. It's the nature of our business. But I have a special reason for getting it over quickly where he is concerned — he's such a sweet man.

Tyson had lived boxing most of his life and, perhaps surprisingly for one with such a

Mike Tyson and Frank Bruno had been good friends long before Bruno's world title fight in Las Vegas.

vicious street roustabout image, was very articulate and erudite about the sport. One of his favourite stories involved Joe Louis taking less than one round to knock out his great friend John Henry Lewis in the 1940s. The Press at the time were amazed that the Brown Bomber had humiliated his friend in this way, but Louis responded: 'It's because he is my pal. I wanted to make sure as soon as possible that he didn't come to no real harm.'

In interviews after the announcement of his fight with Bruno, Tyson was quick to point out that he thought Frank's rather slow and upright stance would make it easy for him to secure a quick KO, but he was also insistent that Frank had every right to share the ring with him. 'Bruno has been beaten only twice — by Bonecrusher Smith and Tim Witherspoon, and they were both world champions. He's not only got every right to challenge me, but he has as good a chance as any of the leading contenders around. It seems to me that if some people had their way they wouldn't let anyone fight me, which would mean I would have to retire tomorrow.'

Most boxing observers agreed with Tyson. Frank did have the right to the fight, but it was a fight in which he had no chance. Some even said that that the match would put Frank in serious physical danger. Several sports writers revived the old story of Bruno's myopia and his operation in Colombia. They suggested that, even though the operation had been a success, it was a statistical probability that Bruno would suffer a detached retina if he took severe punishment — and all agreed that severe punishment was likely to come from the cruel fists of Mike Tyson. Experts started to look at the way Tyson hit his opponents and some analysed the way he had demolished Trevor Berbick in a display of aggression and ferocity unseen since the days of Rocky Marciano. The prevailing view was that Tyson was the most lethal fighter ever

born and that his punching power was particularly deadly because of the way he rotated his fist on impact. Such a blow in the eye, it was felt, could be all that was needed to end Bruno's career for ever.

But while the experts were ruefully predicting doom, Frank was riding high as the favourite of Joe Public. They loved his 'Know what I mean 'Arry' and his dry one-liners and, although they feared for him, they also hoped that a miracle would happen and that Frank would pull it off. Frank's erstwhile verbal sparring partner Harry Carpenter was no exception.

> He is a professional and it would be a mistake for anyone to try to protect him from others. He believes he has a chance against Tyson and you would not expect him to say anything else. Tyson is the best in the world, but other heavyweights must be given the opportunity to fight him. The only alternative is for them to curl up and die. I remember other champions being described as invincible. No one gave the young Cassius Clay a chance against Sonny Liston. Clay was the 7–1 outsider, and look what happened there. It's a question of how you approach the Tyson power. I don't understand why people go at him. That is playing his game. He wants them to walk into his punches. The only way to have any chance is to back off, run away for five or six rounds and make him miss. Mike is an immensely strong young man, but if you can avoid his punches who knows what might happen? Bruno can box, he has a height advantage and he can hit hard, too.

As excitement mounted and the gloom-and-doom merchants fought to outdo each other with dire predictions, the Bruno camp became increasingly frustrated. Four separate dates were set for the fight but, on each occasion, they were changed due to some real or

Frank Bruno, the people's favourite. This publicity shot was taken after Frank had been voted Britain's Best-Dressed Man in 1988.

imagined crisis in Tyson's build-up. Certainly Mike and his promoters had their problems. The champion was involved in a car crash that knocked him out; he re-broke his hand; he was involved in a street fracas and in an acrimonious divorce battle with his wife.

Bruno was affected by these delays and they began to wear down his patience. 'It's

time Mike Tyson got his affairs in order,' he fumed. 'He is either breaking his hand, smashing his car or having a divorce and I can tell you it's getting me down a bit. I know he is champion, but he is not God.'

Meanwhile, Mickey Duff and Jarvis Astaire were battling to get the now much-battered contract, signed in August, back into shape. The original deal was that Tyson would defend his title in Britain in October 1988 but, as that date came and went, it became increasingly obvious that Tyson wanted to stage the fight in the US and the back-room negotiations, which included the powerful American cable network Home Box Office, became heated and protracted. The end result

Mike Tyson greets Terry Lawless at a pre-fight Press conference in Las Vegas. Promoters Mickey Duff (centre background) and Don King (right) help to build an atmosphere for the big occasion.

of all the wheeling and dealing — not only over the venue, but also about the Monopoly amounts of money involved — was that the fight would be staged in Las Vegas: and it was there, despite some further delaying hiccups, that it took place finally in February 1989.

Bruno did not win a round in the fight; he was put to the canvas within 15 seconds and out of the fight by a seven-punch sequence in the fifth that had the referee moving in before Terry Lawless could throw in the towel. Yet Bruno came out of it with honour, his plucky Brit status intact and the love and admiration of his fans strengthened.

Despite being overwhelmed by Tyson, Bruno had rocked the champion with a devastating left hook towards the end of the second round. It was a moment which had the pulses of British boxing fans racing. Even Lloyd Honeyghan, who was watching the fight from ringside, said: 'At that moment I thought Frank was going to do it.' But Tyson was too

strong and too savage and, although he admitted later that no one had ever hit him harder than Bruno, he was never really in any danger.

Bruno himself was devastated by the defeat. He was close to tears for the first 20 minutes after the fight but, when composure came, he was severely self-critical in his comments to the Press.

> I feel ashamed I lost. I feel so sad. I did what I had to do, but it just wasn't enough. So many things run through your mind when you're in the ring waiting for Tyson. Then he just comes swarming all over you. It's difficult to put that pressure into words. There's a lot of weight on your back. A lot of people were running me down. I knew if I was beaten in the first round they would all say I had bottled it. When I did go down it was a surprise more than anything. I didn't really get hurt. It's my pride that hurts the most.

Later, as the Press pestered him for his plans for the future, Bruno was more thoughtful. 'I want to forget about boxing for a while. I'm only 27 and I don't really want to give it up, but I've got other plans in my life.' It came as no surprise to those who knew him that those plans included a gradual rebuilding of his determination to succeed in his dream to become world champion, and marriage, finally, to his long-time, and fiercely loyal, girlfriend Laura.

PREVIOUS PAGE *Bruno can't duck low enough to avoid a powerful right from Mike Tyson.*

RIGHT *After the disappointment of the Tyson fight Bruno returned to England and his family to reconsider his plans for the future. Frank and Laura with Frank's mother, Lynette, and their two daughters, Rachel (left) and Nicola.*

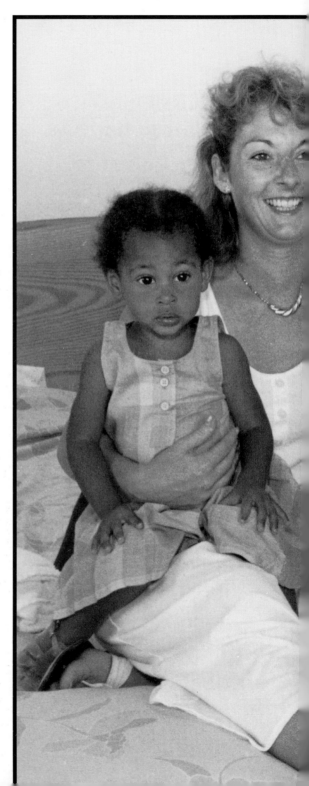

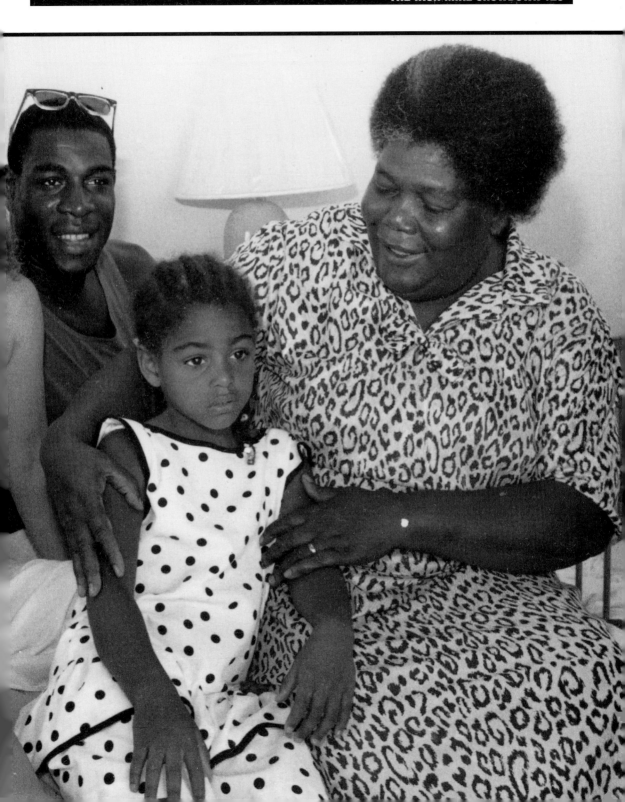

MARRIAGE AND REBUILDING THE DREAM

Back in the hotel after the Mike Tyson defeat, Laura Mooney cradled Frank's head in her arms and begged him to give up fighting for a living. His mother had made a similar plea earlier and the Press were unanimous that this

After ten years Frank and Laura tie the knot. The wedding turned into a media affair and as many as 3,000 well-wishers crammed into the streets outside the church to share in Frank's joy.

was the time for Britain's favourite boxer to hang up his gloves. But Frank would not be rushed into a decision and he asked Laura to give him two months to think about it before making up his mind. In fact, it took considerably longer than that.

It was more than two and a half years before Frank Bruno got into the ring again. He settled back into his quiet routine of training, enjoyed the limelight, pantomime and HP sauce advertisements and, in February 1990, took Laura to the altar at their local Roman Catholic church in Hornchurch, Essex.

It had been ten years since Frank first met Laura, ten years which had seen the birth of daughters Nicola and Rachel and which had cemented the inter-dependence of Frank and Laura into a rock-solid union. He was never really happy when he was not with his family and she was only really content when she was looking after him. Both had said that marriage would come in time; and the right time came during Frank's slow recuperation from the Tyson fight.

Frank becomes a TV star — HP Sauce were the beneficiaries as sales rose dramatically.

THERE'S NO MISTAKING HP's PUNCH.

Frank and Laura are introduced to Princess Diana at the premiere of the film Steel Magnolias. Frank's association with the Prince and Princess of Wales was well established through his unstinting work for the Prince's Trust.

They had planned a small wedding but thousands of fans turned up, including Harry Carpenter, who flew back from the Commonwealth Games in New Zealand to be there, and the ceremony became more of a media event than the quiet and personal commitment they had envisaged. But it didn't dent their obvious happiness. Frank was infectiously joyful. 'It was beautiful, beautiful. I'm a happy man. I don't know why

Two and a half years elapsed before Frank returned to the ring after the Tyson fight. Instead he tried his hand at entertainment of another form – pantomime with Little and Large.

it took me so long.' Among the mountain of wedding gifts was a set of silver napkin rings from the Prince and Princess of Wales. Frank had, for many years, been unstinting in the work he had done for the Prince's Trust; work that, along with his efforts in the ring, had led to his proudest moment outside boxing, being awarded the MBE: an honour he was to receive from the Queen the following week.

While all this was going on, the boxing side

One of the proudest moments of Frank's life. He shows off the MBE he received from the Queen at Buckingham Palace.

of Frank's life was developing at a very slow pace and it was not until November 1991 that he stepped into the ring for his come-back fight against the Benelux title holder, John Emmen. It was, hardly surprisingly considering Bruno's long lay-off, an unchallenging return, but it was felt that

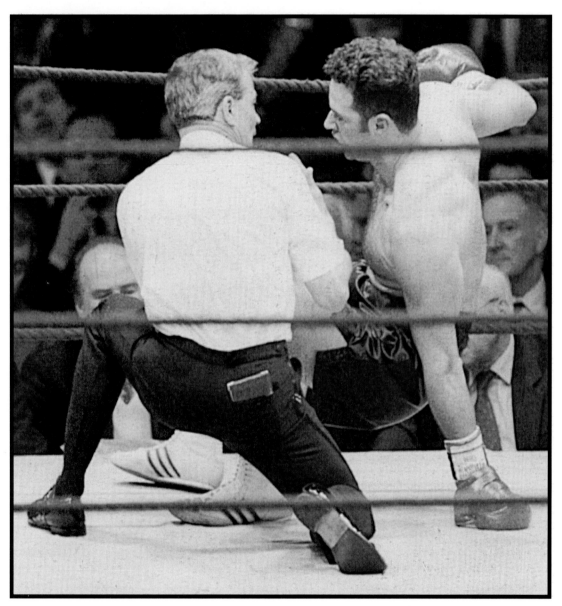

Emmen had the credentials for the job. Even the British Boxing Board of Control had satisfied themselves about the opponent's suitability. 'I've looked at Emmen's record,' said Board secretary John Morris, 'and talked to members of the European Boxing Union's ratings committee, and all of them say he's a

Frank returns to the ring for the first time since his defeat at the hands of Tyson. His opponent, the Benelux title holder John Emmen, proved to be no match as Frank despatched him in the first round.

character and a personality on the Continent. If Frank needs a test at this stage, he's the right one.'

Right he may have been, but he proved to be no match and Bruno put him away with apparent contempt in the first round. It was too quick a win to brush away any ring-rust and it did nothing to answer the questions about Frank's readiness or hunger. But his next fight, some five months later, certainly did.

This was against the very experienced Cuban American José Ribalta at the Wembley Arena. Ribalta had gone ten rounds with Mike

An aggressive Frank sees off the threat of José Ribalta in the second round. The contest produced some of his most clinical boxing.

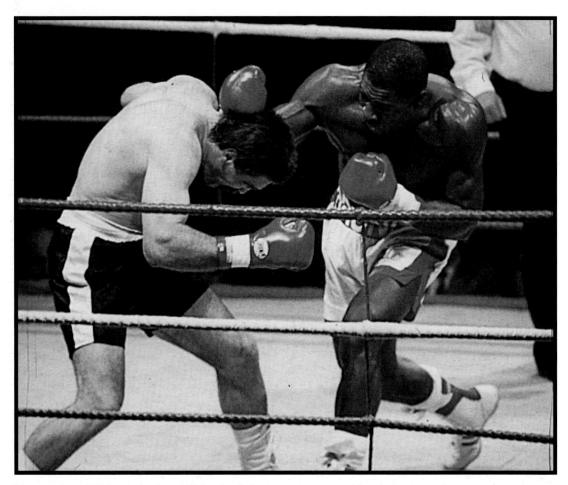

Tyson in 1986 and, in 1991, had been unluckily outpointed by the number one contender for the world title, Pierre Coetzer of South Africa. He was, all agreed, a stiff test for the still far from match-fit Bruno, but Frank produced some of his most efficient and clinical boxing to inflict the first knock-out Ribalta had suffered in a 40-bout career.

Just over halfway through the second round, Frank steered Ribalta to a neutral corner and threw a big right to the Cuban's head. Ribalta was knocked half out of the ring and, even though he was unable to get back, Frank continued his attack until the referee stepped in.

Frank's jab finds a way through the Pierre Coetzer defence. He used every trick in the book to stop the South African in eight rounds. It was a side to him which had not been seen before.

It was a great win for Bruno, certainly his most positive performance for some time, and it had the Press shouting the 'Our Frank is back in contention' anthem. Frank, too, was delighted. 'That final punch felt really good. I am a lot more mature than when I fought Tyson. This guy was an incredible opponent. It is stupid to say it wasn't a test — when a man says he is going to blind you, you don't waste any time. I was especially delighted because of the things he had been saying before the fight, but now I have to sit down with Mickey Duff and see just how far we can go.'

No one knows just how much talking they did, but it was not long before Duff announced that Frank was to fight South African Pierre Coetzer on October 17 and that he had applied to the International Boxing Federation to have the fight recognised as a world heavyweight title eliminator.

It was a tough one for Frank. Coetzer, at 31, had worked his way into contention with 17 straight victories which had won him a title eliminator against Riddick Bowe. Bowe won that fight, but Coetzer was still highly rated and had openly stated his hunger to brush Bruno aside so that he could have another crack, this time against Evander Holyfield.

In the event the match showed Coetzer, and the world, a completely new Frank Bruno. He used every trick in the professional's book — some said every dirty trick in the book — to stop Coetzer in round eight. He barged, he pushed, he leaned, he held, he hit low, he elbowed and he shoulder-charged the South African into submission: and the crowd loved every second. At last, they said, our Frank has grown up. He has learned how to mix it in the ring and he has learned the tricks of the trade used by other professionals. Mr Nice Guy had a mean streak — hooray.

But Coetzer had no complaints. His considered opinion after the fight was simple: 'He's strong and he hit me hard — it's as simple as that.' And his manager, Alan Toweel, was impressed. 'If Frank fights like that in America, he could well do it. This is the way to do it. If you get an American ref he turns a blind eye to those tactics. A performance like this would frighten Americans.'

Bruno liked to hear this and his own reaction to the 'dirty' smears was typically no-nonsense. 'I never go in to fight dirty, but I've got to protect myself. Believe me, it's not table tennis in there. You've got to do what you can to win — it's a serious business.'

Serious business may it be; serious money certainly. Now even more money loomed large on the horizon with the tempting prospect of yet another shot at the elusive world title. The game was on again, but the big one was still a year away. With the heavyweight division in a mess and with mega-buck negotiations taking place in smoke-filled rooms on both sides of the Atlantic, Frank had to stay sharp — and that meant another fight before the title shot.

Carl 'The Truth' Williams was the target this time, and Bruno beat him in a brutal slog that had very little to do with boxing; at least on his part. Frank again used fair means and foul to overcome the more skilful Williams. Williams ducked and weaved and boxed and looked good against a lumbering Bruno, who seemed to offer the American an easy target. Both men suffered damage: Frank needed five stitches and Williams looked as though his face had been pumped up with compressed air.

The fight was won, if that is the word, by Bruno's clubbing right hand, but it was not pretty and it was unsatisfactory, even for Frank. 'I was trying too hard to knock him out from the first round. I've obviously got a lot of things to work on. I need to sharpen up and loosen up, but I know I have got a lot of the rust out of my system. I think I have the power now to beat Lewis.' Lennox Lewis was then the British heavyweight champion of the world.

RIGHT *Third time lucky? Frank prepares for his third attempt to capture the world crown — a fight with Lennox Lewis which was promoted as the biggest money bout in British boxing history.*

Bruno's next fight was to be every boxing promoter's fantasy: a world heavyweight championship battle between two Britons and on British soil. It would be the biggest money bout in British boxing history, and it was set for Cardiff Arms Park in November 1993. It was expected that the fight would gross £18,000,000 and attract up to 82,000 people. Even at this stage, however, it was assumed by the pundits that Bruno had no more than a puncher's chance against Lewis. They felt that Bruno was inordinately lucky to be getting a third shot and they had little sympathy for the tough, some said greedy, talking of the Bruno camp over money.

Out in the real world, however, the hype market was building up apace. Bruno was going to hammer Lewis for calling him a 'White Slave'. Lewis charged Bruno with being an imposter on the world championship scene. 'I'll knock him out in three,' he boasted, and there were few around who didn't believe him. And why not? Lewis was younger, as fit, if not fitter, and full of the self-confidence that comes with champion status. He was also universally regarded as Bruno's master when it came to the more technical and subtle crafts of boxing. Lewis, the majority held, was going to give Frank a boxing lesson. As one journalist wrote in his paper's big fight special: 'The local brew in Cardiff is not Tetley's or Whitbread but Brains — and Bruno is about to have his scrambled.'

Henry Cooper had Lewis 'a class above Frank'; Tommy Morrison, the WBO champion, said that Bruno 'would not be able to cope with Lewis' speed'. It seemed all the experts were writing Bruno off except Lewis

A Lewis left hook connects with a bruised Frank. Despite the pre-fight bravado, Lewis knew that you could never count Frank out of a contest.

himself. In a brief moment of rationality during the flurry of chest-beating, he said: 'You can never count Bruno out until he is on

Lewis feels the full impact of a Bruno jab. Frank was ahead on points after the first six rounds until Lewis finally broke through his defences in the seventh to end Bruno's hopes once again.

his backside.'

And that, of course, is just where Frank went — but not with ignominy. As in his other championship fights, he left the ring with his head held high. He had held his own comfortably for the first six rounds and was ahead on points on many cards, but in the seventh he dropped his guard and took a

massive left hook to the jaw from Lewis. From that moment Bruno was out of it. He was still on his feet but he was no longer thinking about the fight — it was as though his brain was in another county. Lewis, as any professional would, took full advantage and landed as many as 20 full-power shots to Bruno's head while he stood defenceless. The big man had no counter and the referee had to step in quickly to save Frank from what would certainly have been serious damage.

The dream was shattered again.

The dream might have been over for the time being, but Frank can leave the ring with his head held high after the Lewis fight.

FOURTH TIME LUCKY

No sooner had Bruno left the ring after the Lewis defeat than the familiar calls for retirement began to increase in volume: this time led by his mother Lynette. 'I don't want Franklin to take any more punishment. He has taken enough already. I know he has this burning ambition to bring home the belt, but it is obvious that the Good Lord does not want it to be. It would be best if from now on he concentrated on taking care of his wife and my two beautiful grand-daughters.' It was a plea that found a sympathetic response everywhere. Even the Press were unanimous. Bruno's time had come; his dream could never be achieved and the truly sensible fighter would see the signs, recognise the dangers and call it a day.

Frank, however, was having none of it. This time there was no two-and-a-half year delay before he went back into the ring.

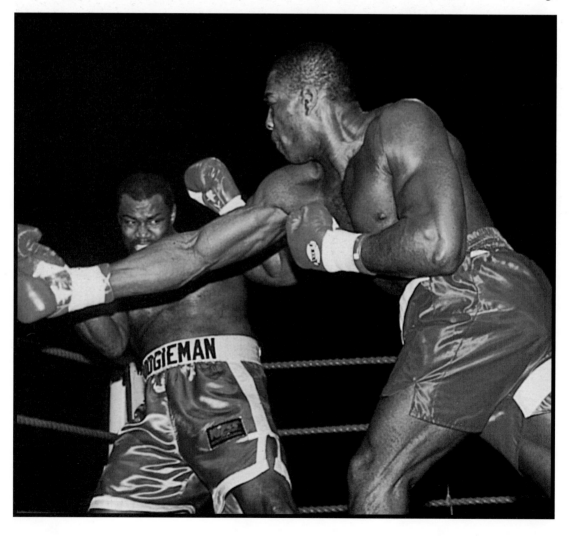

Negotiations began almost immediately and, just five months after the Lewis battering, he was in the spotlight again, against American Jessy Ferguson. Mickey Duff had brought Jessy 'Boogieman' Ferguson from Philadelphia as a hand-picked confidence-booster for Frank but, as so often in the past, the fight was a farce: pure pantomime. Ferguson was 36, out of condition, had lost 11

Carpenter was aghast. 'It was a pathetic performance and there are thousands of people who paid up to £100 for a ticket. I don't think any of them will be satisfied by that.'

And yet Bruno, who was held to be doing his usual less than sparkling best, was not targeted by Fleet Street's big guns — that honour was kept for the Lawless, Duff and

LEFT *A quick return for Frank proved to be yet another fiasco as he clubs Jessy 'Boogieman' Ferguson into submission in the first round.*

An unconvinced Harry Carpenter quizzes Frank after the Ferguson fight. Meanwhile, the attention of most of the media was focused on Bruno's promoters, Lawless, Duff and Astaire.

of his 31 fights and was plainly a fall guy. He was designed to make Bruno look good, but in the event achieved the opposite.

Bruno failed to land a clean punch throughout, but clubbed his inept opponent into submission in the first round with a series of apparent rabbit punches to the back of the head and neck. Even his friend Harry

Astaire management triumvirate. Their general feeling of disgust is perhaps best summed up by the Daily Telegraph's Steve Bunch, who wrote at the time:

Boxing is a sad and dirty business where the ability to make loose ends meet is a prerequisite — and Duff and Astaire are past masters at connecting loose ends. They do nothing illegal but for 12 years they and their client [Lawless] have relied on willing fans and somebody at the BBC with more money than sense. The trio have enjoyed over a decade of lucrative Bruno fights but only two out of 37 victims were ranked in the world's top ten. It has been 12 years of frantic hype punctuated by three unsuccessful world title challenges. It has been year after year of hand-picked flops and former contenders, each with no more ambition or chance of survival than a balloon in a hurricane.

Incriminating stuff, but it fell on deaf ears. Even as the shells were bursting, Bruno's management were busy making plans for yet another lucrative fiasco. Ostensibly the effort was being put into getting Bruno a fight against British-born Michael Bentt, who held the low-prestige WBO version of the heavyweight title. In the event Frank's next appearance in the ring, nearly a year later, was against yet another no-hoper has-been in Rudolfo Marin.

The fight took the same pattern as before: a clumsy, inelegant, static affair which the referee had to stop, in Bruno's favour, early in round two. It was a fight that changed few minds. Bruno was now being regarded as something of a has-been himself; a caricature boxer appearing occasionally for his payday before a perpetually gullible public. Few now regarded him as a serious contender for

Back to business as usual for Big Frank as he despatches Rodolfo Marin within 65 seconds. Yet Bruno still failed to persuade the boxing Press that he had any more to offer in the big time.

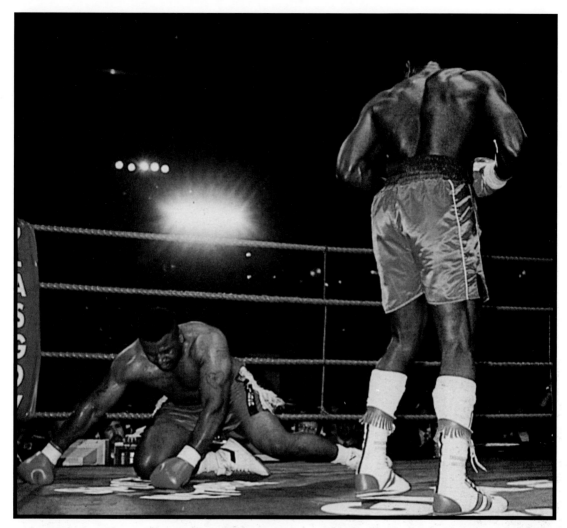

anything and many felt embarrassed that the big man was being made to look a fool.

Amazingly, the pattern repeated itself three months later when, at Kelvin Hall in Glasgow, Bruno was pitched against the 19-stone immobile statue Mike Evans. As before, Frank rained steam-hammer shots on him for six minutes and Evans went home with a few bob in his pocket, but no friends.

There was a difference this time, however. Almost unbelievably this ridiculous matching of Britain's favourite against a giant

Frank topples the 19-stone giant Mike Evans during their fight at Kelvin Hall in Glasgow. Again the bout was a predictably one-sided affair.

cardboard cut-out earned Bruno yet another world title shot — this time against the immensely experienced WBC title holder Oliver McCall. Credit for guiding Bruno to his fourth title shot must go to new manager Frank Warren, who had replaced the out-of-favour Terry Lawless, but the prevailing

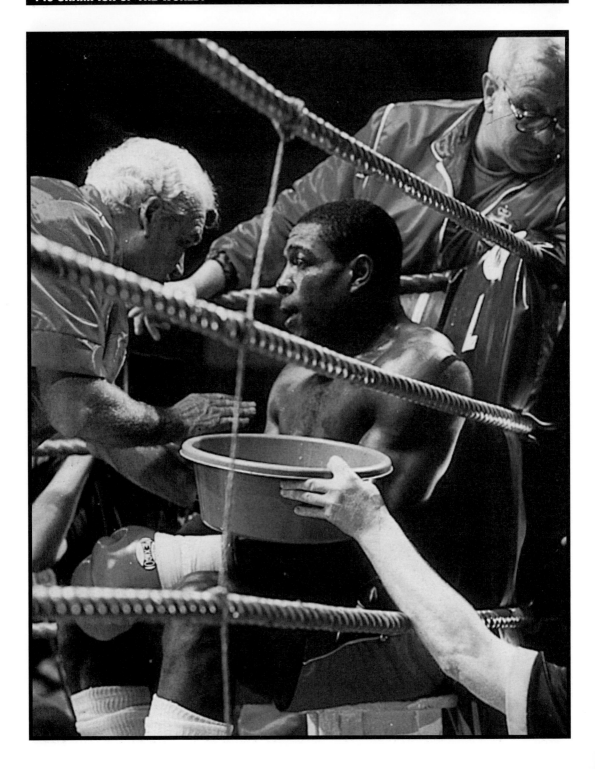

LEFT *Frank receives instructions from his corner during the Evans fight. Amazingly, victory here was to give Frank a fourth shot at the World Heavyweight crown, this time against WBC champion Oliver McCall.*

sentiment on the championship matching was incredulity. How could the strong, popular but lumbering Bruno even dare to hope for success against the experienced, crafty and tough McCall? Bruno, again, would listen to none of it: 'I don't care what people are saying, I've got my chance and that's all I care about.'

Defeat was unthinkable for Frank. He knew it would certainly spell ignominious retirement and that the public would not stand for yet another come-back. He also knew that

victory would see Don King, the American promoter who, with Frank Warren, was now controlling his business dealings, pulling out all the stops to get him another crack at Tyson before Lennox Lewis, who had been beaten by McCall. It was, without doubt, a heady prospect. Frank never doubted that the odds were with him. He had sparred against McCall when he was preparing for Tyson and he had handled the big American well. 'His style suits me down to the ground,' he said. 'He's shorter than me and he's lighter than me. I feel I have got the better jab and the better

The men who put the fourth title chance together. Don King and Frank Warren parade their contender at a Press conference to announce the McCall fight.

right hand and I know that in the last nine years I have become much more mature, much stronger and much more focused.'

It was talk that pleased the public, but the incident that had them flocking once again to his corner came from the mouth of the incredibly crass McCall. Gerald McClellan, a friend of McCall's, had suffered brain damage

ABOVE *Frank with close friend Nigel Benn at Wembley Stadium. Their association took on added significance in the light of McCall's comments about Gerald McClellan.*

RIGHT *True Brit. Frank remained resolute to finally capture the World Heavyweight crown for himself and his country.*

when losing to Nigel Benn in a WBC super-middleweight title fight. McCall, at a Press conference, said: 'I'll take Bruno out and try to do to him what Benn did to my friend Gerald. That's the way I feel. This isn't a sporting event, I am going in with bad intentions. The only reason I took this fight was because of Gerald. This isn't about my world title, it's about vengeance and revenge.'

The savagery of these comments led to calls for the Boxing Board of Control to act in the interests of boxing. This was more than the traditional, and often entertaining, pre-fight hype; it was an awful and near-criminal statement of intent that damaged the sport. It also elevated Bruno to white knight status and gave him that extra incentive, if any were needed, to get his own back in the ring.

Frank had another reason of his own for wanting to win: a new member of the Bruno family. He had always wanted a boy and wife Laura had duly obliged at the beginning of the year when she gave birth to baby Franklin. Frank was deliriously happy. 'At the end of last year I said I had two burning ambitions for 1995 — for Laura to give birth to a boy and for me to win the world title. I have got my first wish with Franklin, and now I am going to make the second one come true. I

Frank lands a left jab in an early round against Oliver McCall (below). The onslaught continued late into the fight (right) until McCall rallied in a desperate bid to save his title, but Big Frank managed to hold on.

have never lost the dream and I sincerely believe it is my destiny. I am desperate to win.'

On September 2, 1995, a red-letter day in British boxing history, Frank Bruno did just that. Under the lights of the Wembley Arena the man who had tried, tried and tried again rose like the phoenix and, carried along by a tidal wave of emotional support, achieved his life-long ambition: he became the Heavyweight Champion of the World. After 13 years of graft, disappointment, criticism and frustration, the nearly-man of boxing became a winner — but it wasn't accomplished without the odd flutter of the heart.

On the night Frank outboxed McCall for much of the fight but the fans knew he had done that against Bonecrusher Smith, Tim

PREVIOUS PAGES
RIGHT *The dream becomes a reality. Nigel Benn raises an exhausted Frank to his shoulders as Frank Warren and rising star Naseem Hamed join in the celebrations.*

LEFT *And the winner . . . an emotional Frank, complete with belt, salutes the Wembley crowd. Years of perseverance and inner conviction had finally come to fruition. Those who had doubted could doubt no longer. Frank Bruno was WBC Heavyweight Champion of the World.*

Witherspoon and Lennox Lewis, and gone on to lose. Frank's habit in long fights had been to run out of steam and most feared the same would happen again. McCall, though outfought, was unhurt and he did unleash a ferocious assault in the final minutes which had the audience and the television millions holding their breath. But Frank had learned something from those earlier defeats. He had learned how to hold and to smother and he used these new skills, for skills they are when legs turn to jelly and the body is exhausted, perfectly. In what was an almost unbearably tense last round McCall just could

not get through. He flailed wildly in a last desperate attempt to win but Bruno dug deep and held the charging bull at bay. McCall finished the stronger and seemed to be getting through the Bruno defence but, when the final bell sounded, Bruno was still standing proud. He knew he was world champion and you could feel his pride at the back of the arena.

Frank won his championship by a unanimous points decision — 115–113, 117–111, 117–111 — and the lovable trier of British sport basked in deserved adulation. It was, after all, a triumph of dedication, perseverance and years of inner conviction. The British Press, for so long yearning for a winner, pulled out all the stops. The tabloids produced six- and eight-page spreads and the victor deserved all of their fulsome praise. Frank Bruno had finally proved himself: our one-lining, hard-punching, pantomime buffoon was having the last laugh. He was the Heavyweight Champion of the World.

The British public were given the opportunity to congratulate Frank, when a parade through the centre of London was staged in his honour.

ABOVE *The pride in daughter Rachel's expression at the post-fight Press conference says it all. Frank had really given the media army something to cheer about.*

RIGHT *'I did it for you son.' A proud Frank holds up baby Franklin, the son he had always wanted. Now that he has won the World Heavyweight crown, are there any ambitions left?*

FRANK BRUNO'S PROFESSIONAL FIGHT RECORD

1982

Mar	17	Lupe Guerra	W	KO	Round	1
Mar	30	Harvey Steichen	W	RSF	Round	2
Apr	20	Tom Stevenson	W	KO	Round	1
May	4	Ron Gibbs	W	RSF	Round	4
June	1	Tony Moore	W	RSF	Round	2
Sept	14	George Scott	W	RSF	Round	1
Oct	23	Ali Lusaka	W	KO	Round	2
Nov	9	Rudi Gauwe	W	KO	Round	1
Nov	23	George Butzbach	W	Rtd	Round	1
Dec	7	Gilberto Acuno	W	RSF	Round	1

1983

Jan	18	Stewart Lithgo	W	Rtd	Round	4
Feb	8	Peter Mulendwa	W	KO	Round	3
Mar	1	Winston Allen	W	RSF	Round	2
Apr	5	Eddie Neilson	W	RSF	Round	3
May	3	Scott Le Doux	W	RSF	Round	3
May	31	Barry Funches	W	RSF	Round	5
July	9	Mike Jameson	W	KO	Round	2
Sept	27	Bill Sharkey	W	KO	Round	1
Oct	11	Jumbo Cummings	W	RSF	Round	7
Dec	6	Walter Santemore	W	KO	Round	4

1984

Mar	13	Juan Figueroa	W	KO	Round	1
May	13	Bonecrusher Smith	L	KO	Round	10
Sept	25	Ken Lakusta	W	KO	Round	2
Nov	6	Jeff Jordan	W	RSF	Round	3
Nov	27	Phil Brown	W	Pts	Round	10

1985

Mar	26	Lucien Rodriguez	W	RSF	Round	1
Oct	1	Anders Eklund	W	KO	Round	4
Dec	4	Larry Frazier	W	KO	Round	2

FRANK BRUNO'S PROFESSIONAL FIGHT RECORD

1986

Mar	4	Gerrie Coetzee	W	KO	Round 1
July	19	Tim Witherspoon	L	RSF	Round 11

1987

Mar	24	James Tillis	W	RSF	Round 5
June	27	Chuck Gardner	W	KO	Round 1
Aug	30	Reggie Gross	W	RSF	Round 8
Oct	24	Joe Bugner	W	RSF	Round 8

1989

Feb	25	Mike Tyson	L	RSF	Round 5

1991

Nov	20	John Emmen	W	KO	Round 1

1992

Apr	22	Jose Ribalta	W	KO	Round 2
Nov	17	Pierre Coetzer	W	RSF	Round 8

1993

Apr	24	Carl Williams	W	RSF	Round 10
Oct	1	Lennox Lewis	L	RSF	Round 7

1994

Mar	16	Jessy Ferguson	W	RSF	Round 1

1995

Feb	18	Rudolfo Marin	W	KO	Round 1
May	13	Mike Evans	W	RSF	Round 2
Sept	2	Oliver McCall	W	Pts	Round 12